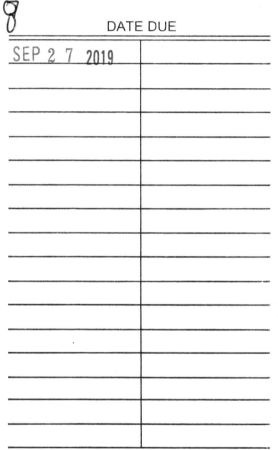

DATE DUE

SEP 2 7 2019

DEMCO, INC. 38-2931

Legends *of* Animation

Genndy
Tartakovsky

Legends of Animation

Legends *of* Animation

Genndy Tartakovsky

From Russia to Coming-of-Age Animator

Jeff Lenburg

CHELSEA HOUSE
An Infobase Learning Company

Genndy Tartakovsky: From Russia to Coming-of-Age Animator

Chelsea House
An Infobase Learning Company
132 West 31st Street
New York NY 10001

Library of Congress Cataloging-in-Publication Data
Lenburg, Jeff.
  Genndy Tartakovsky : from Russia to coming-of-age animator / Jeff Lenburg.
— 1st ed.
      p. cm. — (Legends of animation)
  Includes bibliographical references and index.
  ISBN-13: 978-1-60413-842-9 (hardcover : alk. paper)
  ISBN-10: 1-60413-842-4 (hardcover : alk. paper) 1. Tartakovsky, Genndy,
1970– —Juvenile literature. 2. Animators—United States—Biography—Juvenile literature. I. Tartakovsky, Genndy, 1970- II. Title.
  NC1766.U52T375 2011
  741.5'973—dc23
                          2011026688

Chelsea House books are available at special discounts when purchased in bulk quantities for businesses, associations, institutions, or sales promotions. Please call our Special Sales Department in New York at (212) 967-8800 or (800) 322-8755.

You can find Chelsea House on the World Wide Web at
http://www.chelseahouse.com

Text design by Kerry Casey
Cover design by Takeshi Takahashi
Composition by EJB Publishing Services
Cover printed by Yurchak Printing, Landisville, Pa.
Book printed and bound by Yurchak Printing, Landisville, Pa.

Printed in the United States of America

This book is printed on acid-free paper.

All links and Web addresses were checked and verified to be correct at the time of publication. Because of the dynamic nature of the Web, some addresses and links may have changed since publication and may no longer be valid.

To Edna, Jacob, and Abby,
this one is for you and there'll
be a test in the morning.

CONTENTS

ACKNOWLEDGMENTS

First and foremost, my sincere thanks Genndy Tartakovsky for his cooperation in taking time from his busy schedule and sharing his stories and memories that provided great insight into his journey to becoming an animator and a beloved figure and force in the animation industry.

Furthermore, this book would not have been possible without the contributions of many individuals and organizations. In particular, my special thanks to CalArts; the Margaret Herrick Library of the Academy of Motion Picture Arts and Sciences; Arizona State University Fletcher Library at the West Campus; Fullerton College Library; Joe Swaney, Cartoon Network; Shareena Carlson, Cartoon Network Studios; and Turner Home Entertainment for their kind assistance and for providing material, including articles, books, histories, transcripts, and illustrations, important to the success of this project.

In addition, I wish to thank many publications and news organizations whose source material was invaluable in researching and writing this biography, namely *The Christian Science Monitor, Daily Variety, Entertainment Weekly, The Los Angeles Times, The New York Times, USA Today, Variety, The Washington Post*, and countless others.

1

From Russia with Love

He has been one of the most influential writers and directors of television animation for more than a decade. With an incredible work ethic and strong devotion to his craft, he has produced some of today's most popular and entertaining comedy, sci-fi, and action-adventure television cartoon series known to legions of fans from around the world, including *Dexter's Laboratory*, *Samurai Jack*, and *Star Wars: The Clone Wars*. For this Russian immigrant-turned artist, the journey has been a long and winding one. His success did not come immediately or without his share of struggles and hardships along the way. For Genndy Tartakovsky, it has been a journey worth taking.

Gennady ("Genndy") Boriosvich Tartakovsky was born on January 17, 1970, to Boris and Miriam, of Jewish descent, in Moscow, the capital, inland port, and largest city of Russia. He was the younger of two sons, born two years after his brother, Alex. Located in Russia's Central Federal District, Moscow was a center of commerce and industry, with navigable waterways, shipping ports, and railroads converging from all parts of the former Soviet republics. Factories provided a major proportion of the country's industrial output. At the center of it all was the symbol of Soviet power and authority: the Kremlin.

11

The imperial residence and governmental seat with its imposing Great Kremlin Palace was adjacent to Red Square.

By trade, Boris worked as a dentist and had his own successful practice. Contrary to some reports, he was neither a member of the Soviet Cabinet nor high-ranking official in the Soviet government. He did, however, provide dental care for Russia's hockey team. Miriam, on the other hand, was an assistant principal at a local school. Due to his successful practice, Boris was able to provide well for his family. In the then Communist-controlled country, they lived in a three-bedroom apartment.

While growing up, Genndy developed tremendous love and respect for his father. Boris was a stern and old-fashioned man, and yet socially, as Genndy described, "the life of the party." As Genndy explained, "He was very outgoing, very funny. He was old-schooled when it came to raising kids—a little bit of that fear factor, but when he played with you, it was great."

Miriam was the one everybody loved the most and the best cook among her circle of friends. "She was like an angel—one of those sweet, sweet people," Genndy said, "who people turned to and she did anything for them. She was great that way."

Genndy's personality is a mix of both of his parents. But overall he is much more like his mother, partly from spending more time with her in the kitchen when he was growing up.

Genndy was born and raised Jewish. Like many Soviet Jews, his family practiced their faith in the face of domestic strife and anti-Semitism. For many years, millions of Soviet Jews and Jewish settlers, trapped behind the Iron Curtain, lived in isolation under the censorship of the Russian government. Many of their predecessors had suffered the grave consequences of openly expressing their bond with Israel and were arrested, fired from their jobs, sentenced to long terms in prison, or exiled to Siberia. In 1967, three years before Genndy's birth, Israel's victory over Egypt, Jordan, and Syria in the Six-Day War only emboldened Soviet Jews. In a brave effort, they took on the Kremlin and its religious intolerance and immigration policies. Many demonstrated, others declared a hunger strike, seeking freedom of religious expression and unrestricted emigration to Israel—and the United States and West Germany—despite facing the severe consequences of arrest and imprisonment. Such declarations attracted others of faith from various cities of the Soviet Union. Soviet authorities tried to persuade world public opinion that the Jewish culture was flourishing in what had long been an anti-Jewish environment. Despite living under these hostile and volatile conditions, Genndy was reared by loving parents who only wanted what was best for him and his brother, and to live and prosper free of such oppression.

By his own admission Genndy had a happy childhood. As a young boy, he was unaware of the extent of the discontent in his socialist country "We were fortunate since my dad was a dentist that we had money, so we had everything we needed," Genndy stated. "We had food and the outstanding things in life like toilet paper. So we were well off. My memories are good."

HEADING TO THE LAND OF OPPORTUNITY: AMERICA

Leonid Brezhnev, General Secretary of the Communist Party, ruled the USSR at that time. He held that title the longest, second only to Joseph Stalin. Under Brezhnev's rule, he dramatically expanded the global influence of the Soviet Union and acquiesced in allowing Jews to leave the country. In light of the pervading anti-Semitism, Boris became concerned that the fact he was so successful would be made an issue by the Soviet government and he and his family would suffer because of it. So, in the summer of 1977, when Genndy was only seven, the Tartakovskys fled the country. "My parents moved because they knew we could not have the same opportunities there as we would have here [in the United States]," Genndy recalled. "The horrors of war were still fresh on their minds and [there was] considerable anti-Semitism."

Genndy and his family left the USSR with their cousin's family and countless other Jewish families, with their ultimate destination being the United States. First they immigrated to Florence and Rome, Italy, where they lived together in cheap housing for three months in a neighborhood of all immigrants. It was a chaotic and unsettling time for them as they prepared for their new life in America. Every morning, immigrant families spilled out on the streets with their suitcases—some had 15 to 20 suitcases with them representing their entire life's possessions—and held a makeshift flea market to sell their wares so they could gather cash to survive and live until they moved on.

"All these immigrants would go out to this area and sell stuff right out on the street," Genndy said. "One of my dad's cousins had this amazing toy train collection, the old Russian and international versions, and sold them for like $500—his prize possession."

Three months later the Tartakovskys relocated to the United States. They made Columbus, Ohio, their new home. Founded in 1834, this capital city, located in the center of the state, featured a diverse economy supported largely by state, federal, and local government offices, educational and research institutions, and manufacturing industries.

His parents rented a two-bedroom townhome and had friends that lived in the city. It was the first time Genndy and Alex had to share a bedroom.

Finding work in his profession was difficult for Genndy's dad. Boris was unable to practice dentistry as his dental license from Russia was nontransferable. To become licensed, he was required to take a dental exam. But with a family of four to provide for, he worked instead as a technician making dentures.

Right away Genndy immersed himself in American culture. His passion for drawing started after buying his first comic book, DC Comics's *The Super Friends*, at a 7-Eleven convenience store in Columbus. *The Super Friends*, the adventures of a team of superheroes, was also produced as a popular Saturday-morning cartoon series, simply called *Super Friends*.

Genndy initially developed his love for cartoons while growing up in Russia, where some classic Disney cartoon features were imported and shown on Russian television. One of his favorite Russian cartoons was the slapstick Tom-and-Jerry-styled *Nu pogodi!* (*Wait Till I Get You!*), featuring the outlandish escapades of a wolf trying to catch a fleet-footed rabbit. Living behind the Iron Curtain, his exposure to

At 26, Genndy became one of the youngest animation directors in the industry helming his breakout cartoon series, *Dexter's Laboratory*, for Cartoon Network. © *Cartoon Network*

American television programs had been limited. They were unlike anything he had experienced in Moscow, whose state-controlled network broadcast mostly news. There was no television culture to speak of like in America. He was amazed by the plethora of programming available. "I just fell in love with television," he told *New York Times Magazine*. "It was like candy: there's 'Wonder Woman,' 'Dukes of Hazard.' And I was a 'Three's Company' fanatic."

His favorite American animation at first was classic Warner Bros. cartoons like those by screwball animator and director Tex Avery, known for his wild and exhilarating style and unabashedly slapstick humor. "I was really drawn to it [cartoons] and drawing," Genndy said. "I had never seen anything like comic books. When I saw my first," he joked, "my head exploded. It was so great."

With cartoons and comics becoming his obsession, Genndy started drawing every day. He copied from comic books and tried drawing original ideas of his own. But he became frustrated at times with his skill level. As he admitted, "I remember I was horrible at it [drawing]. For the life of me, I couldn't draw a circle."

In his opinion, his brother, Alex, was a much better artist than he was. Genndy had the passion but, unlike other kids his age, his drawings were not the kind that would impress anyone. According to Alex Tartakovsky, "Our parents noticed how much he liked to draw, so they brought him to an art teacher. After several classes they asked her opinion, and she said, 'Well, he's no Michelangelo.' What Genndy has in his art is great life. He's not the type of guy who draws vases or a deer."

After a short stay, the Tartakovskys moved to Chicago, Illinois, on the southwestern shore of Lake Michigan. The city was known for its high concentration of European ethnic groups, including Czechs, Croatians, Germans, and Ukrainians. They made the Roger Park neighborhood, in the city's northernmost suburb, their new home.

As a third grader, Genndy attended Eugene Field Elementary School in Park Ridge, a suburb of Chicago that borders the northwestern neighborhoods of Edison Park and Norwood Park, in proximity to O'Hare International Airport. One of its most notable students was Secretary of State and former First Lady Hillary Rodham Clinton, who attended classes there in the 1950s. Genndy went there through eighth grade before graduating in 1985. Already fluent in Russian, he learned to speak English from his studies at school and from watching television. As he added, "I just got hooked, and that made me learn English much faster. . . . When I grew up, if I had a free moment, I watched TV. And I turned out fine."

TRYING TO FIT IN

Genndy had a difficult time transitioning from foreign to American schools, especially grammar school. By how he looked and acted, it was apparent to others he was an immigrant. His clothes were not fashionable, his hair was unkempt, and although he was learning at a fast pace, his command of the English language was still a work in progress. Old attitudes toward the Soviet Union were strong and pervaded American society in everything from television shows to movies. "It was still fresh on people's minds," Genndy professed. "Right now, nobody calls Russians Communists. But back then, it was still kind of fresh. So I definitely got made fun of for being Russian and for being Jewish."

It was hard for him because he could tell others knew he was a foreigner. He suffered from stereotypes of being Jewish. "The kids at school grip onto the easiest stereotype," he told *The Jewish Journal*, referencing his days when he was labeled a Communist. "My parents never tried to hide the fact we were Jewish."

Genndy just wanted to be accepted like anyone else. In fact, he said, "When I moved to America, I wanted to fit in and be American."

In third grade Genndy made some new friends. One of his best friends was Jim Parks. Like Genndy, he loved to draw and they spent most of their time drawing together. Parks was a good artist for his age. He specialized in drawing robots, Genndy in superheroes. At one point they put their sketches together into an album and tried selling their drawings.

As his family's financial situation improved, Genndy went on to attend Chicago's prestigious Lane Technical College Prep School (also known as Lane Tech). The large, coeducational four-year public high school offered a college preparatory curriculum and degrees in accounting, architecture, art, engineering, journalism, medicine, mathematics, music, science, and teaching However, despite its long

Genndy's passion for drawing developed after moving to America and buying his first comic book in the late 1970s, DC Comics's *The Super Friends*. *(Courtesy: Cartoon Network)* © *DC Comics*

history and reputation as one of the area's most outstanding educational institutions, Genndy never felt like he fit in until his sophomore year when he felt more accepted. "I realized I have to hep it up," he said. "I discovered girls. So that was the motivation for everything." As a result, as a teenager, he became preoccupied with watching animated cartoons and continuing to draw figures from comic books, taking several art classes.

Genndy continued drawing throughout high school. But, being that he was in the Midwest, there was really no animation industry to speak of other than small, independently owned, commercial production houses. With Boris now working as a dental technician and Miriam as an insurance clerk, Genndy had no real aspirations that he could get a job for himself doing art. As he explained, "I always convinced myself that I will make independent films. I would go to see the new art and the Music Box Theatre and all the animation festivals. I was exposed to that a lot and I realized then that maybe this is what I'll do. I'll make independent films. It will hit that little bug of mine. I never thought I would move to Los Angeles and get into the industry."

Then, at age 16, Genndy and his family's whole world was rocked by a shocking turn of events. On November 1, 1986, Boris suddenly died of a heart attack. At the time, Alex was already attending University of Illinois in Champagne, about three hours away. The death of their father left some pretty big shoes to fill and resulted in a huge financial void. Miriam earned around $17,000 a year, barely enough to support Genndy and herself. With the help of a friend, they moved into an apartment in government-funded housing that, unlike the projects of Chicago, was in a nice, three-story brownstone building where many elderly people and people on welfare lived. To help make ends meet, Genndy balanced work and his studies. He worked various part-time jobs on the weekends as a cook at restaurants and as an usher at movie theaters throughout high school and college.

Genndy had not given his future much thought. He had decided he was going to follow his brother Alex and enroll as a student at University of Illinois—"just because that's where he went . . . you just follow your older brother," he said. He had a hard time getting accepted, however, as his grades did not meet the university's requirement.

FOLLOWING HIS HEART

In his senior year, Genndy started to do more art. He took a freshman art class that year and did some advertising projects and felt he had a good knack for it. Chicago was—and still is—a huge hub for commercial art and advertising. He decided he would make his career doing commercial art.

His mother, Miriam, always wanted to see Genndy successful. So, after he graduated from Lane Tech, she encouraged him to become a businessman. But he had different ambitions. In the fall of 1988, he enrolled to study advertising art at Columbia College, a noted art and film school in Chicago and considered the largest and most diverse private arts and media college in the nation. Encompassing 22 buildings that sit in the heart of Chicago's South Loop, the school offers an unparalleled array of courses with exceptional technological resources.

Unfortunately, when he enrolled Genndy was unable to get the classes he wanted. Every single art class he wanted was full, and so he did not have any choice over the classes he was given. Instead he had to take core subjects, such as English and Science, that semester and defer his dreams of taking art classes until the second semester. "I was bummed out," he admitted, "I was really looking forward to having college art classes." As with all students, Genndy was required to fill in an elective requirement and noticed animation was included in the list. Excited, he chose that as his elective and took an animation class. From the first day he walked into the classroom, his excitement grew. The lab-styled classroom featured 10 portable light tables for drawing lined up next to each other and he found the whole atmosphere inspiring. "I got goosebumps when I walked in," he said. "I knew then that this was my calling."

After taking the class, Genndy switched to studying film as his major and was instantly hooked on pursuing a career in animation.

One of Genndy's instructors was Stan Hughes, a nurturing independent filmmaker whose specialty was producing scratch-art and under-the-camera experimental film shorts. Hughes had a personal collection of 16-millimeter prints of classic Tex Avery Warner Bros.

Vintage 8mm color film reel of Genndy's favorite Russian animated cartoon growing up, the Tom-and-Jerry slapstick-styled, *Nu pogodi!* (*Wait Till I Get You!*), following the outlandish escapades of a wolf trying to catch a fleet-footed rabbit.

cartoons that he screened for students in class. Genndy loved watching the films and asked Hughes if he could freeze-frame them so he could study them more closely. Genndy patiently ran them through a Movieola, a film-editing machine, to review and analyze them one frame at a time. Then he drew sketches of them—especially of Warner Bros. animator Rob Scribner's inbetweens—to master the laborious, painstaking art of creating character movement in cartoons and to build his portfolio as an animator. Before then, using an oversized VHS video recorder he owned, he recorded every single cartoon that aired on television and watched them, pausing them in still-frame and drawing from them until he wore out all the tapes. Once he attended Columbia and saw how he could control and roll through the actual films, "I really started to develop an analysis of animation," he said, "and how to break it down."

In time, Genndy's drawings showed improvement. But still, in his words, they did not have that "connective tissue" they needed. He was apt at figure drawing but never considered himself talented in the "drawing department." But, with animation, he was driven and kept pushing himself to succeed.

In the spring of 1990, Genndy graduated. By fate or destiny, he believes he was led to the next phase in his journey. Alex's roommate at the University of Illinois was a bright and talented young artist by the name of Rob Renzetti. Two years older than Genndy, he later created the Nickelodeon animated television series *My Life as a Teenage Robot*. Genndy first met Renzetti when he went to visit Alex at school. They never talked about animation but Renzetti, it turned out, was just as much a fanatic of animation as Genndy was. Renzetti subsequently graduated with a degree in art history from the university, where he also produced a student film.

At the end of Genndy's freshman year at Columbia, Renzetti talked to Alex, who said during the course of their conversation, "Genndy is going to Columbia College and studying animation." Renzetti told him, "I know that animation department."

After graduating, Renzetti decided to go back to college. He went to Columbia College at the same time Genndy was still studying animation but never called him to let him know he was a student there. During his second year, Genndy went to his life drawing class. A guy came up from behind him and said, "Aren't you Alex's brother?" It was Renzetti; he was in the same class.

Both enamored of animation, they quickly became good friends. Genndy worked with Renzetti on his student film, adding sound to it, and Renzetti provided moral encouragement in return. The turning point in Genndy's life came after Renzetti handed him a catalog for a famous animation school, the California Institute of the Arts (CalArts), to take home with him. Established in 1961 by Walt and Roy Disney, many people consider it a leading center for undergraduate and graduate study in the performing and visual arts. Thumbing through the catalog, Genndy was amazed to find that CalArts offered some 15 classes in animation alone.

Genndy set his sights on going there. He applied several times but was never accepted. After the first two years of classes, his next two years at Columbia would have been devoted strictly to producing films. Impressed by CalArts's program of classes, Genndy wanted more instruction. Even though he was not sure he could afford it, he and Renzetti spent a year trying to get in. As Genndy related, "I had never even thought about leaving Chicago. I loved the city and my mom was there and my friends and everything."

Genndy and Renzetti both started putting together their portfolios, including many life drawing samples. Along with his application, Genndy sent CalArts an entire shoebox of flipbooks of his work. Although he was at the top of his class at Columbia, Genndy was aware that he still did not draw as well as the CalArts students whose work was featured in the catalog he had reviewed. Therefore, his prospects of acceptance looked dim. On a wintery Friday afternoon in late February 1990, a friend told Genndy's mother that a son of a friend she knew was going to CalArts, but "it was impossible to get in unless you knew somebody." After relaying the conversation to her son, Genndy was "pretty bummed out."

That very same day Genndy received a letter from CalArts. He took it with him as he was on his way to work. After he got into his car, he sat and stared at the envelope for a long time because he knew full well he was holding the fate of his future in his hands. Mustering the courage, he finally opened it. This letter was different from the previous stock rejection letters he had received. Reading through all the gibberish, a single sentence caught his eye as he smiled with joy: He had been accepted.

Genndy did not immediately share his good news with Renzetti. He decided to wait until he was accepted and then celebrate together. Days turned into weeks, however, and Renzetti never received a response from CalArts. Finally Genndy told him, "I got my letter."

Renzetti flipped out. "I can't believe it!" Then smiling, he added, "Congratulations."

Renzetti called CalArts right after that. After reviewing his application and materials, they finally accepted him and the two then really celebrated. Little did Genndy know this would become the start of a prolific career in animation, one that would take him to extraordinary new heights.

2

Making the Grade

In the fall of 1990, Genndy packed his things and moved to sunny Southern California with Renzetti to study animation at CalArts. They roomed together in dorm housing on a campus with a population as large as Chicago's Columbia University—around 5,000 students. The institute, housed in a unique five-story building on 11 lush acres in the booming Los Angeles suburb of Valencia, combined innovation and experimentation with one-on-one instruction by noted industry professionals (many of them legends), all of which Genndy found attractive. For Genndy this was the perfect place to learn and master his craft. It was a decision he never regretted.

His freshman year, Genndy took daytime classes in life drawing, color and design, storytelling, character animation, and the nature of producing animation—from concept to storyboarding, to producing and directing—to learn the essentials about his craft. The faculty of professionals instructing him were at the forefront of animation, including Bob Winquist, then head of CalArts's character animation program, art director (*Pocahontas*) Michael Giamo, and animator director/story artist Eddie Fitzgerald. They provided comprehensive artistic and technical training to help Genndy and his fellow students develop into full-fledged animation artists in both traditional and computer-generated

(CG) animation environments. "My first week, I learned more than I had my whole life about animation," Genndy said.

In addition to his course requirements, he also attended lectures, demonstrations, and screenings as part of CalArts' extensive visiting art series featuring noted animators. Lectures were held at night once a week for up to 10 weeks. His lecturers included Academy Award-winning director (*Tarzan, Surf's Up*) Chris Buck and well-known Disney character animator Glen Keane. During these sessions students were separated into special groups according to their style of drawing—from Disney or Warner Bros. style of animation to realistic to anime. As Genndy stated, "Chris Buck, for example, would draw over your scene and help you— somebody who was super talented—see where you could improve."

During his first year Genndy forged many lasting friendships. One of them was with a budding young animator, Craig McCracken, who hung out with Genndy and Renzetti. Other fellow freshmen he bonded with were Lou Romano, who later made his mark as production design artist on Pixar's *Monsters, Inc.* and *The Incredibles*, and Conrad Vernon IV, best known for his work on DreamWorks's *Shrek* and *Shark Tale*.

All freshmen classes were held on the second floor. Genndy and Renzetti sat opposite of each other in classes they had together and McCracken was close by. As Genndy related, "We really complemented each other's skills sets. Rob and I were animators. Those were our strengths. Craig was an incredible designer. Lou was an incredible film-maker and designer. So it was nice to help each other out."

With two years at Columbia College under his belt, and at two years older than most of his fellow undergraduate students, Genndy admits he acted a little cocky that first semester. He was quickly hum-bled, however, after he put his first drawing assignment up on a wall in Winquist's class. He thought to himself, "Wow, I'm one of the worst people in the class."

"They were all naturally talented. Craig would show me drawings he had done when he was 15 and they were literally as good as any he was doing when he worked professionally," Genndy stated. "Everybody else's drawings were just incredible, too. It was clear to me I was not as good as them. I definitely knew I had a knack for animation and much more experience but realized I had to work ten times harder than the rest of my classmates."

Winquist opened Genndy's eyes to the fact he had room for improvement. He was, in Genndy's words, one of the "the most valuable instructors I had as far as my drawing skills went."

As part of their studies, CalArts further required its students to direct and manage their own projects and produce short films throughout all four years as undergraduates. Genndy wrote, animated, produced, and directed two student films during his time there. In 1990, his first year, for his first student production, he made the 4½ minute comedy short *Muffy Meets the Mafia*. It was a Tex Avery-style cartoon in which a cat saves a lovable, giant dog's life. The grateful hound keeps interrupting the cat's life. So finally the cat flies to Italy and seeks out his Godfather to kill him.

In 1991, his second year, Genndy made his second film. Drawing on his boyhood shenanigans with his brother, Alex, he created what later became the basis for his first highly successful cartoon series, *Dexter's Laboratory*. The film short featured two brother-and-sister characters—a small boy genius (Dexter), preoccupied with science, who creates fantastic inventions in his secret bedroom laboratory, and a blonde pigtailed ballerina (DeeDee) as his nemesis; their mother, clueless about Dexter's underground lab and experiments, was also added to the mix.

Genndy developed DeeDee's character first with the genesis of the film emanating from her character. He drew her for a pencil test assignment that was to demonstrate how a character walked or performed a single gesture. For the assignment he drew a gawky girl (not as tall as his later version) with blonde pigtailed hair, who was bright and dressed as a ballerina for one-, two-, and three-second vignettes of her dancing from the foreground to the background. As he commented, "I started doodling this girl in a ballet outfit and I really liked her and I really wanted to do something more organic and do some dancing animation."

Genndy's drawings of DeeDee—"a dancer full of art" as he described her—inspired him to pair her with a short and blocky little kid brother—or "curmudgeon of a kid"—with an obsession for science as the perfect contrast to his dopey, free-spirited sister. In the pencil tests

Genndy's 1991 student film about a small boy genius preoccupied with science and his blonde pig-tailed ballerina sister was later turned into a seven-minute pilot for Cartoon Network's *World Premiere Toons* program that launched his highly successful series, *Dexter's Laboratory*. *(Courtesy: Cartoon Network) © Cartoon Network*

Dexter was drawn differently than he was later depicted, with large feet, and he walked around morosely.

Dexter was not inspired by Genndy's brainy computer engineer brother, Alex, as has sometimes been reported. A huge fan of cartoonist Bill Watterson's daily syndicated newspaper comic strip, *Calvin and Hobbes*, the relationship of the adventurous six-year-old boy and sardonic stuffed tiger in the strip influenced Genndy in developing his characterization of the relationship between Dexter and DeeDee. "I don't credit that enough," he said, "but it was really a huge influence. The relationship between Calvin and Hobbes was so great, so original. I wanted to build something like that for the two of them [Dexter and DeeDee]."

The pencils evolved into much more—a concept for a cartoon short. Genndy's finished short did not differ much from his later successful Cartoon Network series, although "it [the later series] was much better obviously," he admitted. "Storywise, it was essentially the same."

At year's end Genndy's film and Renzetti's student film were among the best student films selected and showcased at the CalArts Producers Show. Many animation producers from Hollywood and from around the world attend the screenings. One of Genndy's friends in his classes was the great Disney animator Sergio Pablos, a native of Barcelona, Spain. He invited one of the producers from Warner Bros. Animation, who was looking to hire animators for a new animation series they were producing, to come out. The producer liked both Genndy's and Renzetti's films and hired them.

BREAKING IN

After graduating in the spring of 1992, Genndy and Renzetti were paid salary plus room and board to work at Blue Pencil Studios in Madrid, Spain, where most of the animation was outsourced. They were two of eight animators on Warner Bros. *Batman: The Animated Series* (at first simply known as *Batman*). Part of FOX's Saturday-morning *FOX Kids* lineup, the half-hour action series revamped the classic caped crusader from DC Comics fame and spawned a new technique in animation using black backgrounds that was eventually dubbed "Dark Deco," with its visual style based on artwork of producer Bruce Timm. Thrown into the fire his first day, Genndy wanted to, as he stated, "hit it out of the park" at his first professional job. He liked the show and he liked the design. But working in the labor-intensive, crank-it-out, assembly-line of television animation proved extremely challenging and made him feel under qualified.

"It was extremely difficult to draw. The drawing level alone was complex. The animation had to be a little more economical and you had to know how to work fast. You had to know how to do your scenes quickly, to start the scene, and know exactly what you had to do," Genndy said. "You had quotas. We were doing between 20 to 40 feet a week. For students coming out of CalArts and jumping into that footage quota is very difficult compared to if you go to Disney, you are going to do between three and a three-and-a-half feet [a week] on feature animation."

In June 1992, while he was in Spain, Genndy's mother, Miriam, died of cancer. The fact he had such a close relationship with his mother made being continents apart after her passing all the more painful and difficult. Genndy immediately wanted to come back to the United States, but his brother, Alex, consoled him and said, "No, just continue. Mom would have wanted it that way." It remained hard for him afterward to continue working and living in a strange country.

After working on five episodes, Blue Pencil Studios went bankrupt at the end of 1992. They owed Genndy something like $2,000 in pay. He and Renzetti decided not to leave and looked for other work. There were a few prospects for animation jobs, but they were months from starting up. So, in early 1993, with no immediate opportunities at hand, they returned to the United States. They bunked with their friend Randy Myers, who had also been a student in one of their CalArts classes, at his apartment in Valencia.

Genndy contacted one of the producers at Colossal Pictures, an independent animation studio in San Francisco, who he remembered liked his student films. They hired him to do some commercial animation. Unsure of how long his employment would last, he lived with one of his best friends' cousins' uncle's family in the heart of San Francisco and started working on commercials. He met and worked with some really talented people—director Mike Smith and animators Ed Bell (best known for his animation on Charles Barkley and Michael Jordan commercials) and David Feiss (who later created Cartoon Network's *Cow and Chicken* series and its spin-off, *I Am Weasel*). They were animating several Pepsi commercials for Colossal. Working as a glorified assistant, Genndy mused, "My job was ruining the commercials."

Actually Genndy was responsible for tweaking and revising the animation as needed. A case in point: In producing one of the Pepsi commercials, Bell, a terrifically gifted animator, animated a scene of a cow in the foreground and a silhouetted family comically pulling up and getting out of a car at a house behind it. Genndy learned much about the strength of good animation from Bell as his timing in his scenes "was so great, it always got a laugh."

A few days later Bell brought Genndy the same scene to work on. "I have a revision from the studio on that," he said.

Surprised, Genndy said, "The scene was great. What's wrong?"

"Yeah, it's *too* funny. You need to tone it down."

Genndy did as Bell asked and modified the timing of the scene to make the powers-that-be happy, even though, in his eyes, it was perfectly executed.

The job itself lasted only a few weeks. Overall, Genndy found working at Colossal a worthwhile experience. "I learned a lot," he confessed. "I bonded with Ed. Mike Smith took me under his wing a little bit."

FORGING AHEAD WITH A PURPOSE

During a hiatus between projects Genndy made the choice to seek something more steady and permanent. After struggling financially in Spain and never getting paid, and with the high costs of living in San Francisco, he went back to Los Angeles. At the time his friend Craig McCracken was already working as an art director on a new animated television series, called *2 Stupid Dogs*, created by Donovan Cook for Hanna-Barbera Cartoons and Turner Program Services. Needing more people to work on the series, Cook, who was coproducing it, asked McCracken if he knew any other experienced animators that were right for the job. Remembering his mutual CalArts alums, he told him, "Rob and Genndy."

McCracken showed Cook their films and portfolios, and Cook hired them as storyboard artists. As Renzetti later reflected, "We had all developed the same tastes together coming from Cal Arts, and we were all influenced by the same kind of stuff. Genndy has an amazing work ethic and an incredible instinct for what is or isn't going to work. His sense of timing and editing is second to none."

In 1993, Genndy was hired as a sheet-timing director to work on his first prime-time animated series, *The Critic.* (*Courtesy: Teletoon*) © *Columbia Pictures Television*

2 Stupid Dogs was part of a successful revival of Hanna-Barbera's fortunes under the leadership of former MTV and Nickelodeon branding veteran and the studio's new president, Fred Seibert. His mission was to reinvent the studio and *2 Stupid Dogs* was his first series in that effort. Teaming up with Seibert to coproduce the program was Larry Huber, who later executive produced Cartoon Network's *What a Cartoon!* series. After taking over the reins, Seibert wanted to restore some of the luster the Hanna-Barbera brand name had lost, as the studio had not had a major television hit since *The Smurfs* in 1981. He told his development people, "There are two things I'm really interested in seeing personally while you're doing whatever work you do—because I have no idea what a development department does. But I'm interested in people you think are fantastic. And in this case I'm interested specifically in animators you think are fantastic with ideas, not writers, and I'm obviously interested in properties you're really thrilled about that you don't necessarily feel fits the system, whatever the system is."

That is when Cook came along with *2 Stupid Dogs*. Seibert immediately signed off on the series after seeing only half of a storyboard in a meeting with him. "I enjoyed it; it had a sly sense of humor and was a real change of pace from most of what was on at the time," Seibert later remembered.

Pairing it with a brilliant revival, *Super Secret Secret Squirrel*, Seibert stuck with the old Hanna-Barbera formula of three cartoons per half-hour, with the classic character as the middle cartoon during each broadcast. Produced and animated at a break-neck pace and tight schedule to turn them out, the production offered "no time to think," as McCracken recalled, other than to focus on "what is best here?" As he added, "I just had to get something down on paper and turn it in."

Working with McCracken, Renzetti, Miles Thompson, and Paul Rudish (the first person hired as an art director of the revamped *Secret Squirrel* and who recommended McCracken) in a portable trailer in the studio's parking lot, Genndy went on to create some of his best-known work on the series that helped launch his career. Doing storyboards as opposed to animating posed an altogether different challenge. He and Renzetti created boards for each episode—a series of cartoony drawings representing the action and story—for the first season. He enjoyed the opportunity it provided him to tell gags and tell the story the way he thought it should be done. McCracken recognized his importance to the series. As he later recalled, "I'm not much of an animator myself, as far as animating goes. I'm more of an art director, more of a story guy, whereas Genndy is a true animator."

On September 11, 1993, *2 Stupid Dogs* premiered on TBS Superstation and was successful. Genndy worked only on the series' first 11 half-hours and 22 10-minute adventures. He left the series as he had a difficult time working as a storyboard artist since Cook "kept changing all of my stuff. I became frustrated because I never really knew if my stuff was going to work or think it was going to work." One area he had issue with was the walk cycles (i.e., walking, running, shuffling, skipping, hopping, jumping, swimming, and other cyclic actions shown in a sequence of drawings) that he had to create in storyboarding the animation of the characters. He was really unhappy with them and took it upon himself to create his own. He showed them Cook. He really liked them and said, "Do you want to animate the main title?"

Consequently Genndy animated the main title in the opening of the program. That first season, he proposed and suggested changes that Cook approved, such as creating new mouth cycles. Slowly he assigned incremental bits of animation to create for series bumpers and one special character modeled after Warner Bros. legend Chuck Jones's The Dover Boys characters from his 1942 *Merrie Melodies* cartoon, *The Dover Boys at Pimento University or The Rivals of Roquefort Hall*. He also became more involved in handling the timing of the animation—deciding how fast characters in scenes move and considering the tone of the animation, as well as the physical traits of the characters, all important elements in storytelling. "I did this specialty stuff and started doing more timing," he said, "and I still felt that animation was my strength."

Although not making great strides, Genndy considered these small steps to be in the right direction and worked hard to keep improving. While making progress in the company of so many talented people, he heard Film Roman Productions had a new animated series that was starting up, called *The Critic*. He applied there and they originally wanted to hire him as a character designer. Genndy felt his skills were not at that level to work as a character designer, so he offered, "I'm kind of interested in doing character design, but I am more interested in doing timing."

Fifteen minutes later they hired him as a sheet-timing director on the series. Premiering on FOX in January 1994, *The Critic* became a breakout hit. Genndy handled animation timing on the first season's entire 13 half-hour episodes. On *2 Stupid Dogs* he had animated a scene where a character dialed a phone—"a nothing scene," as he called it, for which he figured out "really cool timing" that gave the scene great character. For an episode of *The Critic* he was to animate a scene where the critic, Jay Sherlock, dials a phone. Drawing from his experience on *2 Stupid Dogs*, he decided he would use the same timing in that scene since it had worked successfully before. He gave the scene to the director, who said, "What's this? It doesn't work."

Genndy offered to show the director the scene. His timing of the scene got the job done but the director said, "No, no. Just do it normal."

Genndy became flustered afterward. Most prime-time television animations were well paced by their dialogue but the timing followed the same formula—character head bobs, gestures, etc.—never anything too juicy to animate. Consequently in his job he simply plowed through the timing of the animation, doing it in workman-like fashion, but he was not allowed to get creative.

That was about to change, thanks to a promising turn of events.

3

Tooning Out a Television Hit

I n 1995, Ted Turner's 24-hour Cartoon Network launched a nation-wide contest searching for new talent and potential cartoons. Animators from around the country were invited to submit storyboards of their ideas. In the end, 48 animators, both old-timers and fresh young faces, were asked to submit seven-minute pilots that the network would consider for its new revolutionary anthology cartoon series, *World Premiere Toons*. The program revived the traditional cartoon short—six- to seven-minute films, made one at a time, that were once shown in movie theaters before the main feature film—but exclusively for television.

"We are looking for those people, people with a burning passion, artists that are dying to make cartoons—visually driven, funny, with a lot of physical humor kind of cartoons," announced Fred Seibert, president of Hanna-Barbera Cartoons, Inc. The company, renamed in 1996 after Seibert took the helm, was producing the series for Cartoon Network.

Following the time-honored tradition of trying out rising animators and established artists to give birth to new toon stars, Seibert added, "The pinnacle of the cartoon creative process—and subsequently cartoons' best moments—came from shorts."

As Betty Cohen, then president of Cartoon Network, stated to the press at the time, "We hope to create the cartoon stars of tomorrow by allowing hand-picked animators to have free rein over their own productions. . . . This is a gigantic leap toward the fulfillment of a goal we have pursued since our launch—to change the cartoon world in a positive way."

While Genndy toiled away on *The Critic*, Larry Huber, the coproducer of *2 Stupid Dogs*, took it upon himself to show his *Dexter's Laboratory* student film to Cartoon Network's development people: vice president of original production Linda Simensky, and programming executive Mike Lazlo. They were directly involved in the development of the network's search for animators for its pioneering series. The premise of the short quickly won them over.

"When it came in, it was the first fully formed cartoon we had seen," Lazlo said. "It had all the key ingredients you need a cartoon to have—it had a funny premise, it had things you could do in a cartoon and couldn't do in live action. It had funny voices. And, above all, it had genius timing. Genndy has a scientist's version of creativity. A cartoon can't just be a bunch of pretty pictures. In cartoons, you literally have to count frames per second to figure out when something should happen or not happen. He has a gift for that kind of delivery—it's musical. What he really has is art and science together. You never see that."

They approached Genndy and said, "How would like to do a seven-minute version of this—a pilot?"

Excited, Genndy agreed.

While at Film Roman, Genndy set out to give Cartoon Network what they requested. Between completing his work on *The Critic* in an hour or two every day at the studio, he fit in time to storyboard the pilot for *Dexter's Laboratory*. He kept his timing sheets for *The Critic* over the storyboard as cover for what he was doing on company time. A self-professed, rapid Snapple drinker, he had amassed 50 empty bottles and stacked them on his corner cubicle as a makeshift alarm. Every time the producer walked through the door and toward his cubicle, they rattled, giving him enough time cover up his *Dexter* storyboards and act as though he was doing his timing work for *The Critic*.

A poster promoting the 1995 television debut of Genndy's original Cartoon Network *World Premiere Toons* series cartoon, *Dexter's Laboratory*. *(Courtesy: Cartoon Network) © Cartoon Network*

After completing the seven-minute storyboard, Cartoon Network held what they called their "greenlight reviews." This was where animators like Genndy pitched their storyboards in a room full of executives from Cartoon Network and Hanna-Barbera, including Simensky, Lazlo, Seibert, and others.

The entire panel loved Genndy's original storyboard and approved producing the actual pilot, which he completed in early 1995. In this version Dexter and DeeDee fight for control of a shape-shifting device no bigger than a remote control, with a red button in the middle that when clicked turns people into a dinosaur, duck, or snake. DeeDee had taken it from Dexter's secret lab. While all of this is under way, their mother—whose intellect Dexter appears to have inherited—is perplexed as to why neither of them is ready for school. Genndy later added Dexter's and DeeDee's father to the series. He often favored DeeDee because of her athletic prowess but sided at times with Dexter whenever it came down to a battle of the sexes.

By February of that year, 14 out of the 48 animators were hired to develop cartoons using all-new characters for the series. Genndy was one of them. The program gave first-time opportunities to a group of other young artists, including Loyola Marymount graduate Van Partible, creator of the pompadoured rocker and woman chaser *Johnny Bravo*; Craig McCracken, who resurrected his student film *The Whoopass Girls* as a trio of kindergarten superheroes called *The Powerpuff Girls*; Eugene Mattos and Butch Harman, cocreators of the cartoon short, *Short Pfuse*; and Pat Ventura, who wrote and directed *Short Orders*, featuring Yuckie Duck. Participants in the unusual shorts program also included such Oscar-winning old pros as Bill Hanna and Joe Barbera, creators of Tom and Jerry, The Flintstones, and others, in their first solo producing efforts since the 1940s, and Ralph Bakshi of *Fritz the Cat* fame producing a short film featuring a jazz-blowing cockroach.

LEAVING THEM LAUGHING

Beginning on Monday, February 20, 1995, Presidents' Day, at 5 P.M., the results of their efforts were rolled out for audiences with the first cartoon shown in a simulcast on TBS and TNT. Shorts premiered individually once a week starting the following Sunday and then went into regular rotation on the network. The Cartoon Network show was now called *What a Cartoon!*, renamed from *World Premiere Toons*. The first outing to premiere during the three-network "World Premiere Toon-In" event was Genndy's pilot episode of *Dexter's Laboratory*, called "Crime 101." It was followed by the rebroadcast of the animated motion picture *Run for Your Life, Charlie Brown* (1977). (Originally McCracken's pilot for his cuddly, five-year-old superhero girls, *The Powerpuff Girls*, was to air first but did not premiere until mid-March.) The cartoon introduced the short-tempered boy scientist and his prima donna sister, who is every bit as smart as he is but in an opposite direction. Trouble ensued after DeeDee, doing her daily dance of destruction through Dexter's secret laboratory, insisted on driving an odd machine. The result was comical mayhem and madness. The cartoon attracted high ratings in its debut, and audiences and critics craved more.

After its premiere, *Dexter's Laboratory* became the first of the new *World Premiere Toons* shorts to be judged the best and to be developed into a full-fledged series and given its own full-time slot. The pilot was the first to earn the vote of approval by Cartoon Network viewers from around the world who helped the network make that choice. Concurring with viewers who loved the cartoon's humor of the brother-versus-sister relationship, Cartoon Network ordered six additional episodes. In August 1995, *Variety* named Genndy in its 90th anniversary issue one of its "50 to Watch." That September, *Dexter's Laboratory* also earned him his first Emmy nomination for "Outstanding Animated Program (For Programming One Hour or Less)" for the pilot episode, "Changes," for the *World Premiere Toons* series. Consequently, at 26, Genndy became one of the youngest animation directors in the industry.

"The laboratory didn't play a big part in the original version," Genndy recalled in an interview. "But when producers asked me to develop the short cartoon into a series, I needed a way to keep the show interesting. And with science, you can do anything!" So, in the premiere episode, Genndy did just that: He had Dexter invent a remote control that "changes people into animals." He also transferred his own

Genndy's creation of *Dexter's Laboratory* was partly rooted in his child-hood growing up in Chicago, right down to Dexter's parents' suburban home and neighborhood that had a Midwestern flair. *(Courtesy: Cartoon Network)* © *Cartoon Network*

attitudes to Dexter, with the underlying themes being about "a little kid trying to fit in."

Turning the film short into a weekly series, Genndy gave it a Midwest flair right down to the suburban home where Dexter, DeeDee, and his parents lived. Even Dexter's character was partly rooted in Genndy's memories of his childhood in the Midwest. He admits he made Dexter "definitely as a Midwest kid" with a strong work ethic who is not spoiled too much and who loves food and has his own favorite burrito place, "just like I had growing up in Chicago."

In defining Dexter's junior Einstein character, Genndy relied on his experience as an immigrant as well. "Definitely that was a big part of my childhood, wanting to fit in. As an immigrant, you talk funny, you look funny, you smell funny," he added. "I wanted to do nothing but fit in and talk English and sit with everybody else. The one thing about Dexter, if he doesn't fit in, he'll start his own club. He's not afraid to be an outsider. He's much more confident."

Dexter spoke in a German or Central European accent for one simple reason. As Genndy explained, "He considers himself a very serious scientist, and all well-known scientists have accents."

Expanded into a half-hour series, *Dexter's Laboratory* began airing as a regular weekly series in March 1996, with Christine Cavanaugh (who portrayed the voice of the pig in the blockbuster family movie *Babe*) reprising the voice of Dexter. On Sunday, April 28, the show premiered on both TBS at 9:30 A.M. and Cartoon Network at 6:30 P.M. EST. In its February 28, 1997, issue, *The Nation* magazine described the program as "a place where experiments exploded into cartoon craziness. From his laboratory-of-wonders, boy genius Dexter cooks up half-an-hour of hilarity for the kids." In reviewing the series Jacquelyn Mitchard of *TV Guide* called the show "a dandy."

Two short cartoon segments aired between each *Dexter* episode. The first was *Dial M for Monkey,* starring Dexter's superhuman lab monkey, Monkey (voiced by Frank Welker), who fights evil. The second one was *The Justice Friends*, the adventures of three superheroes—Major Glory, The Infraggable Krunk, and Valhallen—a parody of DC Comics's *The Justice League* and the characters Captain America, The Incredible Hulk, and Thor from Marvel Comics's *Avengers* superheroes.

Episodes revolved around the pint-sized, sometimes maniacal, scientist Dexter doing experiments and making inventions in his cavernous secret laboratory (which he pronounces "la-bore-a-torrey," due to his thick German or Central European accent) in the bowels of his parents' home. The lab appears much bigger than their small home and is accessible only to Dexter, by uttering several different passwords or activating hidden switches on the bookcase or pulling out a specific book in his room. Decked out in a white lab coat, blue laboratory gloves, and heavy-rimmed spectacles, Dexter conducted experiments, both large and small, each more outrageous than the last. Some of his experiments included building robots and rockets, switching his brain with that of a mouse, changing his pet monkey into a super monkey, cloning himself and DeeDee, and mutating a large, tentacled monster. In each case, upon completion, the diminutive mad scientist opines, "At last, my greatest work is completed!" On the flip side, when his experiments go badly, Dexter reverts to being a regular seven-year-old kid who becomes vulnerable and anxious for comfort.

Underscoring the series' absurd humor was Dexter's one-sided, intense rivalry with his ditzy, oozing with sugar-and-spice, older sister, DeeDee, who loves ballet over science, loathes books, and believes in fairy tales and superstitions. Despite his obvious brilliance, Dexter never gets the upper hand. He finds his sibling's actions infuriating, especially her uncanny knack for accessing his lab despite his best attempts to keep her out. Becoming involved in his secret experiments, the two often end up in disaster thanks to her sheer delight in playing in his lab and destroying his creations or inventions in the process. In the beginning of the series DeeDee is the only other person to know of Dexter's secret lab, and he manages to keep its presence secret from his ever-cheerful and clueless parents. He is later forced to reveal his lab to them, but they have no memory of it whatsoever after Dexter wipes their memories clean.

Despite his extremely high IQ, Dexter has his share of vulnerabilities. He hates being teased about his size and lack of skill at ball games, despises superstition and popular culture, and always sits at the front of the classroom where he pays rapt attention to his teacher. Because of his lack of interpersonal skills, and his ill temper and arrogance about his science, Dexter does not fit in well with others. DeeDee acts like a true sister, becoming his only link to the "normal" world and protecting him

Dexter, a junior Einstein, cooks up one of his kooky experiments as his ditzy blonde pig-tailed sister DeeDee frolics in the background. *(Courtesy: Cartoon Network)* © *Cartoon Network*

from bullies and rivals. This includes his arch-nemesis, a boy named Susan "Mandark" Astronominov, who tries to take credit for Dexter's achievements and is secretly in love with DeeDee. In later seasons Mandark's character was revamped, becoming more sinister and evil with his laboratory looking dark and spiky; this replaced the bright, cartoony lab featuring the Death Star from earlier seasons. In addition, his plans became nastier and more diabolical. The animosity between Dexter and Mandark intensified after Dexter mocked him for "looking like a girl."

CREATING HIS FORMULA FOR SUCCESS

Week after week Genndy's formulaic *Dexter* won over more viewers in droves. He attributed the character's success to the fact that "Dexter is a dork," he said. "He's part of everybody; the little kid who just wants to do science but who's frustrated. It's what everybody deals with. That's what makes it funny. If you have a character that loses and wins, it makes him more alive."

Unlike more slapstick cartoons from animation's past, like Bugs Bunny, which were originally written for adults and released as the-atrical cartoon shorts, Genndy followed three principles in reaching kids with Dexter: They contained surface physical comedy, some intellectual humor and pop-culture jokes, and overall appealing characters.

Part of the unbridled success of *Dexter's Laboratory* was that it was wholly original while at the same time challenging the perceptions of scientists and engineers. In developing potential stories for the series, Genndy and his team of five animators sat down and reviewed science books, research papers, and the latest science news stories for inspira-tion. For instance, the 1996 discovery of a Martian meteorite containing possible signs of life spawned an idea for a story: Dexter unearths a rock with a mosquito preserved inside. About using science for inspiration, the usually laid-back Genndy said, "I don't mind it too much. I enjoyed chemistry and science experiments as a teen."

Despite such originality, the formidable intellect of Genndy's boy scientist, and favorable reviews, *Dexter* endured some criticisms. Some in the media questioned what kind of role model Dexter was for Amer-ica's youth and the show's influence on children's interest in science. Bryan Reuben of *Chemistry and Industry* magazine wrote that "... the perceived vices of scientists are the flip-side of the virtues of integrity, dedication and concern for the truth. If scientists wish to be seen solely as modest, affable and good fun, then Dexter is bad news. On the other hand, Dexter differs from other cartoon children in that he has a voca-tion. His laboratory gives him status in the sense that he frequently gets things to work. If intelligence, originality and eagerness to learn are virtues, then Dexter is a role model."

In 1996, *Dexter's Laboratory* became Cartoon Network's highest rated program in the United States and abroad (7.5 million people in the United Kingdom watched *Dexter* at least *once* that year). Also, in 1996, the show was voted "Toon of the Year" by Cartoon Network

Genndy masterminds with his pint-sized creation, Dexter, his latest science experiment in Dexter's secret "la-bore-a-torrey" in the bowels of
his parents' home in this publicity photo for the series. *(Courtesy: Cartoon Network)* © *Cartoon Network*

viewers. *Dexter's Laboratory* also won its second Emmy nomination that
year for "Outstanding Animated Program," making Genndy one of
the industry's hottest rising stars. Of his phenomenal success, Genndy

commented to *People* magazine, "It's pretty unreal, but it's Hollywood . . . I'll ride it out and whatever happens next, happens."

Cartoon Network's then-president Betty Cohen was equally enthusiastic about Genndy's meteoric rise and one of cable's hottest properties. "He's got it all," she said at the time. "He's [Genndy] like a big kid in how he seems to understand drama from a child's viewpoint."

Genndy was not the kind of person to take his success for granted. He knew how long others had toiled to achieve the same kind of success or fell short in the process. He was also aware that *Dexter's Laboratory* could be his only shot at fame, so he was willing to put in as much effort as necessary. Pointing to the pronounced indentation of his right index finger used in animating *Dexter*, he told a reporter, "A lot of animators have these things. We call it the index indent, and it comes from drawing so much. The bigger the hump, the longer they've been working."

Despite his success, Genndy never lived beyond his means. He rented a two-bedroom house in Studio City, a Los Angeles suburb, and drove a 1996 Toyota Land Cruiser, and had little time for a social life. Rising at 6 A.M. every day, he routinely worked 60 hours a week in his cluttered studio at the Hanna-Barbera lot in Hollywood. Nonetheless he managed to survive. "I used to eat a lot of burritos," the down-to-earth animator admitted, "but I'm trying to cut down. Lately I've been having a lot of turkey sandwiches and fries."

During his association with Cartoon Network, Genndy became involved in the success of numerous other hit cartoon series that aired on the network—at times working up to 70 hours a week to fulfill his obligations. In 1997, he hired as a writer his old Colossal Pictures's colleague David Feiss for *Cow and Chicken*, a series of comical adventures of a cow and her chicken brother. The series originally began as a single short on Cartoon Network's *What a Cartoon!* series in 1995. But Genndy's principal focus in the months and years ahead was his ongoing commitment to producing new episodes of his hit series, *Dexter's Laboratory*.

"I think it's great that kids identify with the characters," Genndy said at the time.

During the 1998 season, Genndy and *Dexter's Laboratory* made news after deciding to use an idea for an episode submitted by a precocious seven-year-old fan, Tyler Samuel Lee. The Long Island, New York, second grader had submitted an unedited, audiotaped soundtrack of his story, featuring cartoon versions of himself and his mother, made on a $10 Radio Shack recorder. He acted out the characters and even imitated their voices. His false starts are heard, along with the promptings of his mother, Gail H. Hiller Lee, to do his lines, in the background. In his unsolicited story, "Dexter and Computress Get Mandark," Dexter teams up with a personal computer to destroy his laboratory of an archrival. Genndy complimented young Lee on his authenticity and effort behind his idea. "He got all the personalities and the relationships right," he stated.

Genndy produced the episode in the style of a second grader, with crayon-like backgrounds and crudely drawn characters. On April 26, 1998, it debuted on Cartoon Network. Genndy did so without the usual sound effects of a regular show. "It's super-simplistic," he said. "Nothing overpowers the kid's narration. [The scenes] are a little emptier than people are used to."

Lee developed his love for *Dexter's Laboratory* after a friend got him into watching it. He said, "I think I'll watch it for the rest of my life."

Like Genndy's cartoon alter ego, Lee enjoyed performing scientific experiments. He even posted signs on his bedroom door warning his five-year-old sister, Kelsey, to stay out of his so-called laboratory, just as Dexter did with his ditsy older sister, DeeDee.

To be fair, Lee shared the proceeds from the sale of the rights to his story to Cartoon Network with his friend who helped him create it. That included an undisclosed sum of money and boxes of official *Dexter* paraphernalia.

PUFFING UP HIS SLEEVES

In July 1998, Genndy wrote and directed his 53rd and final episode of *Dexter's Laboratory,* entitled "Dexter's Rude Removal." Genndy left the series, returning in 1999, to direct a one-hour special, the Annie

Genndy collaborated with creator and friend Craig McCracken as a writer, director, and supervising producer for two seasons on McCracken's smash-hit Cartoon Network series, *The Powerpuff Girls. (Courtesy: Cartoon Network) © Cartoon Network*

Award-winning *Ego Trip*. Meanwhile he had started working with his friend Craig McCracken as a producer and director on McCracken's latest creation, *The Powerpuff Girls*. The weekly series followed the adventures of three young girls, Blossom, Bubbles, and Buttercup, who accidentally gain superpowers.

As a student at CalArts, McCracken created the characters as The Whoopass Girls in the 1992 short, *Whoopass Stew! A Sticky Situation*, which was selected in 1994 for Spike and Mike's Sick and Twisted Festival of Animation. Later he submitted it to Hanna-Barbera's innovative *What a Cartoon!* show shorts program on Cartoon Network. It was eventually produced as *The Powerpuff Girls in: Meat Fuzzy*

Lumpkins as part of *World Premiere Toons* while McCracken was working with Genndy on *Dexter's Laboratory*. McCracken said his short was the result of "growing up and watching television in the 1970s." The short was chosen as a viewer favorite for two straights years and then commissioned by the network as a series. As with McCracken's original short, the lighthearted, retro-pop, and kitsch-designed program, with its bubblegum colors and anime gimmicks, paid homage to his favorite childhood shows, the campy 1960s live-action series *Batman*, the animated *Super Friends*, and *Underdog*, right down to the conventional format of a battle, a conquest, and a concluding joke in each episode.

"Making *The Powerpuff Girls* was not a difficult decision," said former Cartoon Network vice president of original production Linda Simensky. "Whenever I would speak at a school, people wanted to know when the show was coming out. That was a definite signal."

On November 18, 1998, *The Powerpuff Girls*, starring the red-haired, level-headed leader, Blossom, who inevitably keeps the peace between the impulsive Buttercup and emotional Bubbles, premiered on Cartoon Network. It enjoyed the highest-rated premiere in the network's history. Critics loved it, too. As Scott Moore of *The Washington Post* opined, "Call it sophomoric. (Okay, it was created by a second-year film student.) Call it stoopid (It's that too, in a way.) But Cartoon Network's *Powerpuff Girls* just might be primetime role models for a post-modern feminist world. Or, at least a fun way to pass a half-hour at 8 on Wednesday nights. You go, girls."

Appealing to both boys and girls, thereafter the series consistently scored the highest rating each week for Cartoon Network across a wide range of demographics—from young children to adults. By October 2000, it won the prime-time ratings war on Friday nights among all other cable networks. While the girls battled dangerous, outrageous villains, it was their relationship with each other, alternating between partnership and rivalry, to which most kids related.

In collaborating on the series, McCracken and Genndy were not above borrowing material from each other to let hard-core fans figure out the references for themselves. Crowd scenes occasionally featured

Genndy tells the story of how he and his wife Dawn met, in animated form, in the 2005 documentary short *Genndy's Scrapbook. (Courtesy: Cartoon Network)*

Genndy's Einstein-like Dexter or had snippets of his show-within-a-show, *Puppet Pals*, shown on a television screen. Otherwise their respective characters lived in completely different cartoon universes.

During the first two seasons Genndy worked as a director, writer, and supervising producer of 20 episodes. From 2000 until the series' end in 2004, he sporadically served as a supervising producer on 24 additional episodes. To his and McCracken's credit, *Dexter's Laboratory* and *The Powerpuff Girls* contributed to expanding Cartoon Network's viewership from 12 million to 72 million, an experience he calls "the most unrealistic thing you could think of."

In 2000, Genndy took time to tie the knot. He married a woman who turned his head after he met her on the Hanna-Barbera studios lot. She was a lunch truck operator who made the rounds daily, the brown-haired, strikingly beautiful Dawn David. He later sweetly captured the moment of their meeting and courtship in an animated sequence in *Genndy's Scrapbook*, a 2005 documentary short about his life as an animator included in the two-disc DVD set to his animated series *Samurai Jack*.

Just around the corner, however, awaited Genndy's next crowning achievement, one that came when he least expected it.

4

Jacking Up the Action

In 2001, swapping funny for a fantastical, visceral action epic, Genndy unveiled on Cartoon Network his second animation creation starring his new alter ego, *Samurai Jack*. The series featured a banished, sword-wielding warrior trained as a samurai and transported to the future. Dubbed "Jack" by the locals, he must defeat the evil shapeshifting wizard, Aku, and his robot enemies that bleed oil in action-packed episodes.

Genndy developed the idea after requesting time off from working on the Emmy-winning *The Powerpuff Girls*, and Cartoon Network executives happily obliged. The 31-year-old animator's primary goal in creating a new concept for television was that "I didn't want to repeat myself. I wanted to do something different," he said.

Genndy came up with a six-page pitch that he took to the network that was unlike anything they or anyone else was producing. "It was called *Samurai Jack*, which sounded like it was funny, but it really wasn't set up to be a funny show," Linda Simensky, then senior vice president of original animation for Cartoon Network, recalled. "The truth is, Genndy could have come in with virtually anything and we probably would have said yes."

Instead, his concept was the result of his long fascination with what he called "superhero stuff" from television cartoons he had watched growing up. "There are so many sitcoms, especially in animation," he added, "that we've almost forgotten what animation was about—movement and visuals."

Genndy's latest venture would combine elements of humor to accompany the action. "It won't be like any other animated show on television," Genndy promised in an interview with *Daily Variety* in June 2001, two months before the series' summer debut. "We're using music, cinematic storytelling and very stylized backgrounds to create mood and atmosphere as *Samurai Jack* travels an exotic landscape.

CREATING A CLASSIC CINEMATIC LOOK

One of Genndy's principal influences in creating *Samurai Jack* was the well-known manga series *Lone Wolf and Cub*, written and created by Kazuo Koike and illustrated by Goseki Kojima and first published in 1970. He found it inspiring and sometimes similar in the approach he took with *Samurai Jack* by having a simple story but interesting characters and "cool moods" that are compelling.

In making *Samurai Jack*, Genndy settled on the idea of using a more cinematic look and feel. Calling the series his valentine to cinematic masters like Arkira Kurosawa, David Lean, Sergio Leone, and Alfred Hitchcock, he patterned the high action in *Samurai Jack* after martial arts and samurai films and action movies of the 1970s. In popular samurai films of this period, the action always built to a crescendo during the battles only to be suddenly interrupted by a bit of comedy before resuming. It was a style Genndy hoped to re-create by employing many cinematic techniques popularized in those films, such as the stylistic use of multiple angles and split screens. He also used modern, eye-catching devices, including letterboxing and images shown in three vertical panels, to capture the action and grab audiences. "I think the audience is a lot more adept at looking at split screen from music videos and commercials," he said. "I thought if I brought that to animation it would really make the show more unique."

After taking time off from *The Powerpuff Girls*, in 2001, Genndy returned to television with the high-action epic series for Cartoon Network featuring the sword-wielding traveling warrior *Samurai Jack*. *(Courtesy: Cartoon Network)* © *Cartoon Network*

Classic anime, as in Toei Animation's 1963 film, *The Little Prince and the Eight Headed Dragon (Wanpaku Ouji no Orochi Taiji)*, was another source of inspiration. "Anime always seemed to execute action better than American animation," he told Wired.com. "So when I developed *Samurai Jack*, I wanted great action but through our point of view, and everything followed after that."

Some of the series' thematic inspiration was loosely based on Frank Miller's best-selling graphic novel *Ronin,* right down to, as Genndy noted, the concept of a "master-less samurai warrior thrown into a dystopic future" to battle a shape-shifting demon.

Physically resembling him at least on the surface, Genndy has dismissed the notion that the character of Samurai Jack was a modified fantasy version of his boyhood self and looked like him as a grown adult in cartoon form. "Someone else told me that. I definitely don't think he looks like me. I see him more as a Clint Eastwood type," he stated. "But as an artist, sometimes you can't help yourself. If you're a tall guy, everything is lengthy. If you're short and fat, you draw things that are squat."

What attracted Genndy to the concept was "I've always been in love with samurais," he said, "the kind of classic idea about a hero who has a sword with an intense skill and is very stoic and doesn't talk much. He talks with action."

Making such a transition was not easy. At first, Genndy felt uneasy about doing an action cartoon series after coming off doing comedy. As he told UGO.com, a site devoted to delivering in-depth daily coverage of the latest developments in games and entertainment: "I've always complained about action cartoons. Then I decided that I wanted to do an action and I wanted to do it the way I would want to see one. I thought, 'What if I fell into the same trap?' But I made my list of goals that I wanted to do and stuck with them."

In his opinion, part of the problem with action cartoon series from the 1980s was the characters talked too much, plots were too complicated to tell in a half-hour, and there was "not enough good action." Even though as a kid his favorite from this period was Hanna-Barbera's *Thundarr the Barbarian,* years later as an adult, he realized the show suffered from the same problem: There was little or no action.

Of little concern to Cartoon Network executives was the fact that Genndy and his group were shifting from gag-driven cartoons to make a pure, choreographed action cartoon series. As Simensky once stated, "If you look at *Powerpuff* and even some of the later *Dexters,* they were sort of moving into [action] anyway. A lot of these guys like comedy and they like action, and that's why you get this hybrid—they like both things and they're learning how to fuse them together in cartoons."

Learning from others' past mistakes, Genndy set out to make *Samurai Jack* not only cinematic in scope but to also incorporate everything he wanted in an action series: action, humor, intricate artistry, and minimal dialogue. Combining these elements with his unique visual style and enthralling story lines, he hoped to bring the kind of high energy to the series to make it stand out in the world of action cartoons and give audiences something they had never experience before in animated form on television.

In terms of its animation style, Genndy distanced himself from the late 1950s, heavy ink-line look he used in *Dexter's Laboratory.* Instead he applied the kind of minimally drawn and pioneering, yet

Genndy and his longtime art director Paul Rudish designed *Samurai Jack* in the same sweeping cinematic style of martial arts and samurai films and actions movies of the 1970s. *(Courtesy: Cartoon Network)* © *Cartoon Network*

atmospheric animation style that harkened back to the United Productions of America (UPA) cartoons of the 1950s. He used their style of angular, expressive characters with no visible ink lines against stark, flat backgrounds (painted by background artist Scott Willis).

Reviving the unit system employed by animation in the golden age, where a core group of artists under the supervision of a director produced animated fare, Genndy returned with his core unit intact, including directors Rob Renzetti and Robert Alvarez; storyboard artist Paul Rudish and background designer Dan Krall—all of who had been together since *2 Stupid Dogs*.

Genndy selected actor and comedian Phil LaMarr as the voice of Jack and veteran actor Mako Iwamatsu to provide the vocal characterization of Aku. Putting far greater emphasis on the music scoring than dialogue, he hired *Powerpuff Girls* veteran composer James L. Venable to score the series. After Genndy mentioned to him that the first episode only had two minutes of dialogue, he laughed and said, "OK, well, I guess I'll be doing some work on that."

Venable approached every episode like he was scoring a feature film, composing music for all of the episodes individually as opposed to using what he called "stock themes." He created most of the scores through an electronic sampler, or keyboard capable of duplicating sounds of musical instruments and using only two live musicians— woodwind player Don Markese and himself playing percussion. With the Samurai Jack character often hopping to different countries, sometimes in rapid succession, Venable's greatest challenge was often coming up with appropriate music for each scene. "The trick is to stay somewhere in between what people think that culture's music is and what it really is," he explained.

Genndy was proud of the end result. As he told *The Los Angeles Times* following *Samurai Jack*'s premiere, "From week to week the episodes are really going to range in their scope. The first half-hour is very moody, very serious, and the second episode gets a little sillier. There'll always be a little humor thrown in from behind."

By special arrangement between Cartoon Network and America Online (AOL), AOL subscribers were given a "sneak peek" of *Samurai*

Jack before the series network premiere. The advance look included a sweepstakes offering of a trip to Japan, a peek at first-edition action figures, the chance to play an online game, and opportunity to see behind-the-scenes character model sheets and learn more information about ancient Samurai traditions.

KICKING IT INTO HIGH GEAR

On August 7, 2001, *Samurai Jack: The Trilogy,* a feature-length 90-minute special to kick off the series featuring two 10-minute episodes, officially debuted in prime time at 8 P.M. on Cartoon Network. In the series opener the square-jawed and resourceful Jack comes off like a cross between Bruce Lee and Clint Eastwood, the strong silent type spouting little dialogue, a noble, nimble, tireless hero—a characterization consistent throughout the series. Set in a faraway land, he has his first showdown with the evil shape-shifting wizard, Aku, a godlike monster with crackling flames and eyebrows. In the past Jack's father, a benevolent emperor of Japan, had imprisoned Aku, and Jack's weapon of choice becomes an enchanted sword once used by his father. Aku banishes Jack to a bizarre future filled with flying cars and exotic creatures. Fiercely determined in the midst of his struggles to escape from the time warp and Aku's evil reign, Jack travels to different mystical civilizations and fantastic landscapes, with Aku and his treacherous soldiers lurking around every bend.

Featuring only about two minutes of dialogue in the first half-hour, as Genndy had promised, the most pronounced scenes were two sequences: an emotional scene where Jack, as a young child, is separated from his father by Aku, and a nine-minute montage of Jack being trained in the art of combat—even archery—by various warriors. For the rest of the show Jack relies on his athletic prowess and keen intellect instead of words to get him through every difficult encounter.

The premiere of *Samurai Jack* struck an immediate chord with viewers. Including five subsequent weekend plays on the network, it drew a collective 11.5 million individual viewers, both kids and adults, after a little more than a month on the air.

Intense and stoic, Samurai Jack talks through his actions and skills with the sword. *(Courtesy: Cartoon Network)* © *Cartoon Network*

Critics were equally complimentary. Many liked the show's emphasis on color, action, pacing, and numerous battle scenes and reliance on striking art direction and Venable's evocative musical score. Others had difficulties with the long stretches with no dialogue. Steven Linan of *The Los Angeles Times* bemoaned: "One can quibble with some of the dialogue, which sounds like something you'd hear in *Karate Kid 2* . . . Nonetheless, there is one highly unconventional aspect of the series which sets it apart from others—its willingness to go for extensive stretches in which there is no dialogue." In reference to *The Powerpuff Girls* on which Genndy previously worked, Linan added, "We'd like to see Bubbles, Buttercup and Blossom try that."

Conversely, Anita Gates of *The New York Times* found the series opener "good looking with a pleasing visual starkness, but boring. Small children may feel differently." The series earned a rave review from James Poniewozik of *Time* magazine. In his review, he stated that "in an era of chatty, hyper'toons, this action show knows when to stand still and shut up. Tartakovsky uses generous pauses for drama and laughs, and has no problem going 10 minutes at a stretch without dialogue. . . . You might call *Samurai Jack* a soba western, or sashimi sci-fi. Either way, you'll slurp it up." In her article "New Cartoon Doesn't Seem Quite Right for Kids," *Dallas Morning News* critic Jean Sprier, while admitting the opener was "at minimum captivating, combining aspects of fantasy time travel, heroic legend, and biblical-style struggle for survival," strongly opined that the series was not for preschoolers or "any child susceptible to scary dreams."

Discussing some of the fallout over the scarcity of dialogue, Genndy believed young viewers had no difficulty following the show's story lines. They were "a lot smarter than we've given them credit for," he said, "but we've never given them a chance to figure things out as they're watching television." The fact that he created Jack as decidedly unchildlike for young audiences was intentional. He said, "One of the things I hate about TV for kids is that it condescends to them. A good cartoon is always on two or three levels: surface physical comedy, character appeal, and some intellectual stuff."

Overall, Genndy was pleased with the visual look, set design, and physicality of the animation in the fight scenes. He considered the production of the series "a huge accomplishment" and was proud of the great job his team did in putting it together.

Becoming an immensely popular nighttime fixture, new episodes of *Samurai Jack* subsequently aired on Mondays at 8 P.M. with repeats shown Fridays at 7 P.M. on Cartoon Network, which commissioned 52 episodes during its four-season run with reruns still broadcast today.

In fusing modern cartooning and traditional Japanese art, Genndy struck a perfect balance of moody pacing, visceral action, playful humor, and important morals in every episode. The production itself harkened back to the age-old Japanese culture of silence and elegance, and antecedents of Japanese cinema found in American westerns. Fantastic action mixed with its visual strength added to *Samurai Jack's* cinematic feel. Watercolor-styled backgrounds and minimal use of dialogue, combined with provocative story lines, further underscored Jack's heart-wrenching, hilarious, and thrilling journeys to such locales as beautiful wildernesses and futuristic cities. Anything but predictable, plots were often dark and epic, simple and elemental, and lighthearted. They followed Jack's continuing desire to unearth a device that transported him back in time to his past life while battling Aku and his robotic enemies in the future. In his relentless pursuit, Jack's character is marked by underlying tones of Buddhist honor and respect and honorable actions and thoughts.

Much like its locales and settings, the series' story lines, deeply rooted in ancient culture and history, ran the gamut. In "Jack Remembers the Past," Samurai Jack looks back in time, giving a glimpse of his youth as a young boy who bears a strong resemblance to the character Ogami Itto, of *Lone Wolf and Cub*. Conversely, in "Jack and the Spartans," Jack battles side-by-side with an army of 300 Spartan-like warriors to defend their home from an army of robots, a story inspired by true historical events. On the flip side, "Samurai Quack" spoofs Chuck Jones's classic Warner Bros. cartoon *Duck Dodgers in the 24½th Century* (1953) and pokes fun at the series' stylistic elements and plot devices, like "only ever killing robots and the progressive ripping of clothes" leading to the episode's climatic finish. For added humor, Jack's adversary, Aku, was played by Dodgers' Happy Cat Alarm Clock. Genndy also makes a cameo appearance in the same episode.

With new episodes of the second *Dexter's Laboratory* series (produced by a different production without Genndy's involvement) airing simultaneously on Cartoon Network, sometimes Genndy's characters crossed over. In one *Dexter* episode, Dexter keeps referring to Jack as "Samurai Jaction," saying "That's enough Samurai Jaction for you!" In post-2001 episodes a Samurai Jack action-figure is also prominently displayed on a shelf in Dexter's bedroom.

During all the excitement and swirl of media attention surrounding the series, Genndy celebrated another milestone event in his life. That September, his wife Dawn gave birth to their first child, a son they named Jacob.

In November 2001, New Line Cinema acquired the rights to adapt *Samurai Jack* into a live-action feature film directed by Brett Ratner (of *Rush Hour* film series fame). Genndy, who was to write the screenplay for the film, was exuberant over the news. "I created the show with a cinematic look to it, so it's very exciting to see it actually go to the big screen," he said. "I'm also a big fan of Brett Ratner's films. His sensibilities are completely in line with the feel of 'Samurai Jack.'"

Fans of *Samurai Jack* gobbled up copies of the first DVD that released the following March. It contained the feature-length special that introduced the character along with bonus features, including one series episode, a "Behind the Sword" documentary featuring Genndy, and "The Making of Samurai Jack" from drawing board to television.

Earlier in the month *Samurai Jack* returned for a second vibrant season on Cartoon Network with 13 brand-new episodes. Weighing in on the latest round, *Entertainment Weekly* critic Ken Tucker summed up the show's continuing appeal this way: "No way would Jack have the following it does if it didn't appeal to both children and adults with an eye for art and appreciation of the way pop culture can accommodate different cultural philosophies . . . Tartakovsky oversees an animation style that at first seems crudely simple: static backgrounds and simply drawn figures with a minimum of movement, much like

The 2002 DVD release of episodes featuring Samurai Jack thrown into a dystopic future as he battles with the shape-shifting demon, Aku, was an instant hit with fans. *(Courtesy: Cartoon Network)* © *Cartoon Network*

old Hanna-Barbera-studio cartoons like *Yogi Bear*. But where *'Yogi* and *Huckleberry Hound* looked cheerfully cheap, *Jack* is artful to the point of witty abstraction."

Genndy's stylistic approach drew praise in other high places. On June 8, 2002, during closing ceremonies, the Jury for TV and Commissioned Films at the 26th International Festival of Animated Film at Annecy honored Genndy's *Samurai Jack* (Episode 7) with an award for "Best TV Series." It was one of 245 films from 33 countries screened at the festival. Then, at the annual prime-time Emmy Awards that September, Genndy and his team were nominated for their first Emmy—his eighth overall—for *Samurai Jack* for "Outstanding Animated Program (For Programming One Hour or More)."

After losing for the eighth time, Genndy considered being nominated rewarding enough. "I'd rather be nominated and lose than not be nominated at all," he told a reporter. "A nomination means acceptance by your peers. I don't get caught up on whether I win or lose. Besides, I'll take good ratings over an Emmy any day."

5

Bring On the Clones

W hile writing and directing his highly rated *Samurai Jack* series, Genndy still had hopes of directing a feature-length film that went beyond the conventions of television animation and enabled him to do something on a much larger scale. Bubbling underneath the surface, it was a passion of his he had yet to realize.

In stepping toward that goal, Genndy worked as an animation director on his first feature—a feature-length version of *The Powerpuff Girls* television series written and directed by Craig McCracken—*The Powerpuff Girls Movie*. Produced by Hanna-Barbera Productions and Cartoon Network Movies and distributed by Warner Bros. Pictures, the $11 million, 75-minute fantasy adventure became the first theatrical film by Hanna-Barbera since 1993. It was the only film based on a Cartoon Network series released theatrically.

Opening in theaters on July 3, 2002, it was hoped that the film would appeal to the same base of fans as the hit television series, including kids and families. In this extended big-screen version, Professor Utonium's former assistant, the disgraced monkey, Mojo Jojo, cons the saucer-eyed, superpowered Blossom, Bubbles, and Buttercup into helping him chemically alter the brains of his fellow monkeys and building a grand crystal palace that becomes a military fortress for his

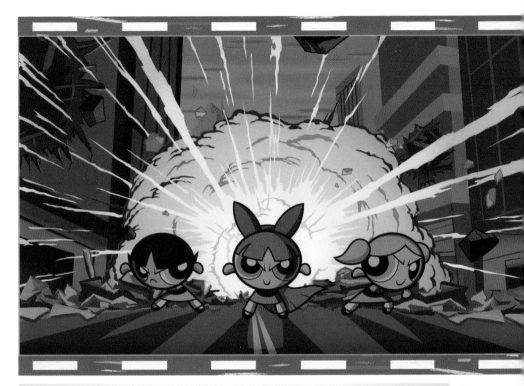

The accidentally endowed superheroes Buttercup, Blossom, and Bubbles storm into action in the feature-length adaptation *The Powerpuff Girls Movie* (2002), marking Genndy's debut as an animation director on a theatrical film. *(Courtesy: Cartoon Network)* © *Warner Bros.*

now evil army of simians and him. The movie is a fable of good versus evil and self-empowerment with the wildly energetic, competitive, and impulsive five-year-olds owning up to their disastrous mistakes and doing battle with Mojo. In the end the girls defeat Mojo and his forces, eradicating them of their special powers.

Newsday critic Gene Seymour gave the PG-rated movie a positive review. As he wrote: "*The Powerpuff Girls Movie* has the right mix of sugar and spice for a satisfying rush." On the other hand, Stephen Holden of *The New York Times* found the girls' tantrum to save the world below the standards of the weekly television series and was not quite so glowing in his critique. As he stated, "Although the film has the wham-bam kinetic fizz of a '60s Pop Art explosion, its hipness quotient is considerably below that of the smartest individual episodes, one of which had dialogue constructed entirely out of quotations from Beatles songs." Others like film critics Roger Ebert and Richard Roeper, hosts of the weekly series *Ebert & Roeper*, gave the movie "two thumbs down" for being too violent in their estimation.

Its opening weekend, *The Powerpuff Girls Movie* performed well below expectations. Competing that weekend with the premiere of the successful sequel *Men in Black II*, it earned a less-than-stellar $3.5 million at the box office and ranked ninth overall. Eventually the movie grossed $11 million in North America and $16 million worldwide, but was a failure. The film—named the "Lowest Grossing Animated Film of 2002" and one of the worst grossing films of all time—was ill timed as the show had lost of some of its popularity by then.

As a result of its lackluster performance, New Line Cinema, fearing the same fate as McCracken's squeaky-voiced little girl superhero film, backed out of its deal to develop a *Samurai Jack* movie based on Genndy's popular television character and series. Despite such a setback, Genndy remained committed, saying, "Jack will come back" and "we will finish the story, and there will be an animated film."

In the meantime events soon took Genndy down a new path, one that would endear him with sci-fi and fantasy lovers and make him a "force" with which to be reckoned. Netting the attention of legendary *Star Wars* filmmaker and creator George Lucas, he would fulfill another boyhood dream. Lured by the distinctive cinematic style of his *Samurai Jack* series, Lucas approached Genndy with an offer to bring that same high-energy, lightning-fast combat, and epic style to television in directing a new animated series based on his successful *Star Wars* film franchise, titled *Clone Wars*.

Bridging the gap between *Star Wars Episode II: Attack of the Clones* (2002) and *Star Wars Episode III: Revenge of the Sith* (2005) of the theatrical film series, the new 2-D traditional animated series would feature material not covered in the *Star Wars* features. It would pick up after the first battle of the wars where *Episode II: Attack of the Clones* left off. As a kid, nobody was a bigger fan of the *Star Wars* film than Genndy was.

"It was definitely one of the first big movies I saw after immigrating to America," he related. "I think it truly is one of the most inspirational, most influential movies of our generation. It certainly inspired me to dream of worlds beyond the here and now."

One month after *The New York Times* rated Genndy's *Samurai Jack* among "TV's Best for 2002" in the field of television animation, animation chat rooms were abuzz after Cartoon Network announced the series in February as part of its overall new 2003 programming—some 400 new half-hours of programming for that season. Genndy would create, produce, and direct the news series in association with Lucasfilm and a team of Cartoon Network studio animators.

Following the news, Genndy stated, "It certainly fulfills one of my dreams to work on a project like *Star Wars*; that is so thoroughly established it has become a part of our culture. It's an awesome assignment and I'm really honored to be a contributor to the *Star Wars* legacy."

The project resulted after a round of talks between Lucas and Cartoon Network to keep "the *Star Wars* property robust and active between motion picture releases." It would not mark the first time the *Star Wars* characters had been turned into cartoons. In 1985, Lucas authorized and executive produced in association with Canada's Nelvana studios the weekly Saturday-morning animated series for ABC, *Droids: The Adventures of R2-D2 and C-3PO*. Lasting one reason, it followed the exploits of the two famous droids with actor Anthony Daniels, who portrayed C-3PO in the *Star Wars* films, lending his voice to character. A year later, the program was repackaged with another ABC/Lucas cartoon series, *The Ewoks*, as the hour-long *The Ewoks and Star Wars Droids Adventures Hour*. *Clone Wars*, however, would become the first animated series starring any of the saga's leading characters. Up to this point they had only been featured in comic books, novels, and video games as well as the blockbuster live-action feature films.

Initially, Lucas thought doing a new animation production for television between future installments of the famed theatrical film series was a bad idea and wanted to do the series only in one-minute installments. Cartoon Network originally approved of Lucas's ideas of doing the series that way. As Genndy recalled in an interview, "They approached me and asked if I would be interested in creating a one-minute program based on *Star Wars*. Well, of course I said, 'yes,' but told them that I couldn't really do anything significant with one-minute episodes—it's simply too short a time to tell a story. They'd have to be at least three to five minutes."

In a conversation with his longtime art director Paul Rudish, who served as art director on Lucas's forthcoming animated *Clone Wars* feature, Genndy said, "This might happen, but I sincerely doubt it. There's no way we're going to do an animated *Star Wars*."

Lucas changed his mind after Cartoon Network executives told him, "We have the team that did *Samurai Jack*, but they want three minutes."

"Oh, I love *Samurai Jack*," he responded, "they can have three minutes." He added that he thought Genndy and his group would "be worthy" of producing the episodes in that format.

TAKING THE PLUNGE

After getting the green light, Genndy was still apprehensive about doing the series even as three-minute episodes. To convince himself whether or not it would work, he whittled down an existing 22-minute *Samurai Jack* episode to a three-minute version to see if it would "make sense, capture the viewer's interest and still tell a compelling story." What he discovered was it actually worked. "I realized it was more time than I thought, but every scene has to say something," he said.

He added, "I found that . . . particularly if each installment worked to build upon the previous one, to offer an important piece to the overall story arc, then end with a cliff-hanger that would inspire the viewer to come back to see what happens next." Despite being only three minutes long, he thought that was enough time to have a beginning, middle, and end to pull the viewer in and make them "want to know more."

After doing the groundbreaking *Dexter's Laboratory* and *The Powerpuff Girls* series, Genndy really wanted to challenge himself. He wanted to do something that was, as he put it, "more cinematic, something on a bigger scale . . . I wanted to see if I could execute it for television."

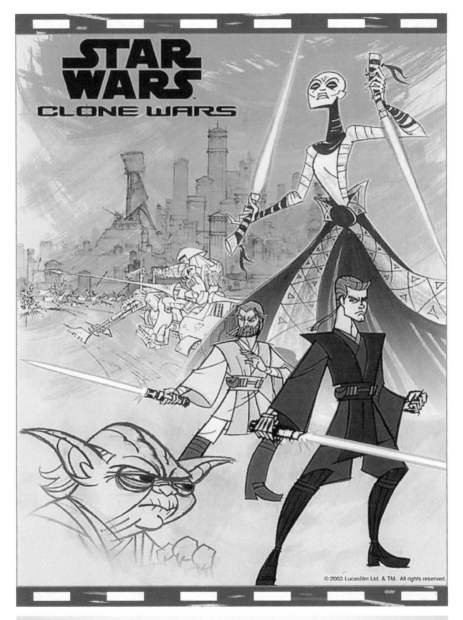

Catching the attention of famed *Star Wars* filmmaker/creator George Lucas, in 2003, Genndy fulfilled another boyhood dream directing a new animated series based on Lucas's successful film franchise, titled *Star Wars: Clone Wars*, for Cartoon Network. *(Courtesy: Cartoon Network)* © *2003 Lucasfilm Ltd. and TM. All rights reserved.*

However, he was nervous about taking on such a cultural icon as *Star Wars*. "It's a huge part of our pop culture," he added.

At first Genndy considered letting someone else do it. But after pondering the idea further, he started to think that leaving the franchise in the hands of others was not such a good idea. As he thought, "What if they make it wrong? Then I would be really upset, and I'd be left with nothing to do but complain: 'Well, *we* should have made it!' So,

Genndy brought the same high energy, lightning-fast combat style of *Samurai Jack* to the *Clone Wars* micro-series told in three-minute chapters. *(Courtesy: Cartoon Network)* © 2003 Lucasfilm Ltd. and TM. All rights reserved.

because I'm a rather aggressive person, I reasoned that I'd better take the challenge myself."

Once he accepted, every member of Genndy's unit was hesitant to take the first steps, including longtime art director, Paul Rudish, again at Genndy's side after working together on *Dexter's Laboratory* and *Samurai Jack*. Genndy called Rudish the kind of art director who could "draw anything, anytime and anywhere without hesitation—he's amazing." But during the first week of preproduction, he was surprised. Rudish experienced what he called "a complete brain freeze" at the drawing board. He was unable to draw a single sketch or palate and, like Genndy, knew the *Star Wars* films better than anyone on his production staff and could easily freehand draw R2-D2, mechanical gadgets and all. "We finally had to take our minds off the enormity of it all," Genndy added, "and just approach this thing like any other project. At last, once we relaxed, it all began to flow naturally."

Lucas's own view of the project was that *Clone Wars* would add an exciting new dimension to the *Stars Wars* saga, offering new characters, epic battles, and intricate stories in short serialized form. As a result, many favorite *Star Wars* characters—Anakin Skywalker, Mace Windu, Obi-Wan Kenobi, C-3PO, and R2-D2—would appear in cartoon form without getting into the relationship between Anakin and Queen Padmé Amidala's characters featured in the movies. As Genndy said, "[Lucas] said to stay between ['Episodes] II' and 'III' and stay away from the love story, and that was it, to focus on the wars." Consequently, he dropped an idea he had for a scene in an episode during a quiet moment during the war where Anakin took out a small hologram picture of Padmé and reflected on how much he missed her. The only outward displays Padmé showed was waving goodbye to the young Skywalker in the first episode and later in the series.

The only characters Genndy and his crew changed were two villains, Durge, an armored bounty hunter, and Asajj Ventress, a bald, female assassin with two pink light sabers. "We just did what we would want to see as fans and as filmmakers," Genndy explained. "All [Lucas] changed was a few planet names and locations."

It was important to Genndy in doing the new series that it appealed to a younger audience and to longtime *Star Wars* fanatics. So he worked very hard to get it right to satisfy both groups. "*Star Wars* always worked for a younger audience and older audience," he said. "I was 7 when the original one came out, and I still loved it. That's one of the most amazing things about *Star Wars*—it works for all age groups."

Of the original characters, he considers Han Solo and Chewbacca his favorites. From his perspective, he loves how they do both comedy and action, and "the personality of a rebel pirate is an attractive one," he added. Another attractive element for him is that the *Star Wars* movies have humor and "wherever we saw that it could fit, we put in a joke" in episodes of *Clone Wars*.

Mostly out of Lucas's respect for his work, Genndy was given free reign over the creation of the series and story lines. The famed producer gave him his seal of approval with Lucasfilm keeping their hands off during the creative process. "Everyone felt they could trust us to handle the property with the appropriate care and concern it deserves," Genndy noted. "So we went away and developed our own story line, a new perspective and approach, along with character designs and production elements—all of which really excited us—and we brought it back and pitched the new scenario to them. And fortunately, everyone really loved it.

Composed of so many different shorts segments in each episode, Genndy approached making *Clone Wars* like HBO's popular series *Band of Brothers*, as a showcase of "several days in the life of." The tone and story arc of the series would be established in the first few episodes starting with "The Battle of Muunilinst," an all-city planet under attack by the Imperial separatist movement. Any research they did to write stories, unlike *Dexter's Laboratory* that involved researching math and science, came from watching the older *Star Wars* movies for inspiration. Genndy and crew did not do any other research. Having seen the movies multiple times, the famed saga and characters had become like "a second language to us," he said.

Teaming up with Genndy to produce *Clone Wars* was a talented group of production artists, technicians, and animators. They included supervising producer Brian Miller; director of production Jennifer Pehl-phrey; storyboard artists Bryan Andrews and Mark Andrews; art director Scott Willis, who shared art direction with Rudish; and various designers, such as Todd Frederiksen, Andy Suriano, and Lynne Naylor-Reccardi.

Production of the series was achieved mostly through traditional 2-D cel animation created at the Cartoon Network Studios in Burbank and overseas with some computer-generated—or CGI—animation produced by Rough Draft Studios in Korea. The studio animated spaceships and the high-action dogfights in space that are a great part of the *Star Wars* film series. In producing the micro-series, Genndy and his team were able to use other signature elements of the *Star Wars* film, including Lucas's Skywalker Sound, to create sound effects and background elements. Every single sound effect in *Clone Wars* was derived from the Skywalker Sound library used in the first five movies, along with some newly created sounds that resulted from mixing two or more different sounds used in the film together. Even Oscar-winning composer John Williams's classic *Star Wars* compositions were featured in the new series.

As Genndy later stated, "I was amazed that when the tapes came back to us from Skywalker the whole show suddenly seemed 'legitimate.' I mean it had the same recognizable sounds as any one of the feature films. We simply couldn't have reproduced this sound on our own."

DEVELOPING THE RIGHT LOOK

One of the most difficult challenges for Genndy and his animation team in the beginning was deciding whether to create animation renderings of the characters that closely resembled the actors in the *Star Wars* films or more like caricatures of them. Rudish's preliminary sketches, in Genndy's words, "didn't come out right—they didn't look like the essence of the character they were supposed to be."

"We played with the style a bit to make it fit," Genndy explained, "but the biggest problem was: Do we caricature the actors (from the *Star Wars* films) or do we caricature the personalities in the movies?"

Young Anakin Skywalker and Jedi knight Obi-Wan Kenobi wage battle using their signature light-sabers in a promotional poster for Genndy Tartakovsky's *Star Wars: Clone Wars* series. *(Courtesy: Cartoon Network)* © 2003 Lucasfilm Ltd. and TM. All rights reserved.

After a series of experimentations, he and Rudish discovered the right look: character drawings that more closely resembled the real actors who played the legendary characters on screen. "It became less about how does Ewan McGregor (the actor in *Episode II* and *Episode III*) look and more about how does Obi-Wan Kenobi look as an animated character," Genndy said. Even then, his animated take on the franchise's famous characters were drawn in Genndy's usual jagged-line look.

Besides making the characters look authentic, Genndy was also concerned that they sounded it as well, like those portrayed in the *Star Wars* movies. Outside of casting Anthony Daniels, the original actor who played C-3PO, he signed on actors who had never appeared in the theatrical film series. Amazingly they were able to create vocal characters that sounded remarkably close to their live-action counterparts.

In producing and directing the series, Genndy drew from his signature style in *Samurai Jack*, incorporating some of the same cinematic techniques inspired by his love of '70s cinema. This became evident in his direction of lightning-fast combat, extended sequences of explosions, sweeping epic vistas, and no dialogue. In some episodes he used 40 or 50 poses or movements in fight scenes, as opposed to most television shows that use anywhere from 5 to 8 and feature films that use only 10 to 12. "If you go and compare them to any other show, ours stands above because our fights are fluid, the timing is very strong, and you see everything but also feel it," he explained. "Even in live-action movies, you don't have as much choreography as we do. Those extra poses really make a difference. You feel the action in the fight much more than you would if it were cut! cut! cut!"

On Friday, November 7, 2003, the first of 10 chapters of the epic micro-series debuted on Cartoon Network, airing weekdays at 8 P.M. ET through November 20, and repeating at midnight. (On November 10, Cartoon Network's United Kingdom action-adventure and anime channel, *Toonami*, started airing it as well.) On Friday, November 21, all 10 chapters aired on Cartoon Network, interspersed throughout that evening's programming, giving fans the chance to see them all in succession. Thereafter the new prime-time franchise was telecast on Friday evenings from 7 P.M. to 12 midnight (ET, PT) as part of its popular Friday night lineup. Episodes were also simultaneously shown on Cartoon Network and Lucasfilm *Star Wars* Web sites.

Interestingly, Chapter 10 of *Clone Wars* aired on the same night as the final episode of Genndy's long-running smash-hit, *Dexter's*

Laboratory, which bowed that evening with its last three original episodes, "They Got Chops," "Poetic Injustice," and "Comedy of Feathers."

The *Clone Wars* series tells the story of the young Skywalker—a student of Jedi Knight Obi-Wan Kenobi, who questions Skywalker's maturity but not his abilities—as a pilot and his rise to power. Narrated by the master Yoda, episodes take place during the epic Clone Wars as he and the valiant Jedi Knights battle the Republic's Clone Troopers across the galaxy. In bridging the story of the film series, Kit Fisto, a Jedi heading a special aquatic unit of Clone Troopers, leads an amphibious assault on the water planet of Mon Calamari. Meanwhile Count Dooku, the leader of the Separatist movement, is joined by a fierce female warrior trained in the ways of the Sith. The rapid-fire action takes place in new locales as well: on the planets Coruscant, Muunilinst, Mon Calamari, and Rattatak.

Visually the style of *Clone Wars* resembled *Stars Wars'* live-action counterparts more than coming across as a continuation of Genndy's *Samurai Jack* series. After Genndy had been working with the same crew for 12 years, the cinematic styling and look of *Clone Wars*, while using some of the characteristics of '70s filmmaking, represented a giant leap forward for Genndy, dispelling any worries viewers had of him tackling a property that they revered so highly.

In fusing two worlds—Lucas's original and Genndy's version, *Clone Wars* produced incredible overnight ratings and high ratings thereafter. Immediate reaction was mostly positive from hardcore fans and critics alike who loved the action and portrayal of the characters. As Phillip Wise of *Star Wars* fan Web sites theforce.net and www.rebelscum.com raved, "I love the look and feel of it, though I was very skeptical when I initially heard how short the episodes would be." Writer Robert Lloyd of *The Los Angeles Times* believed the conventional cartoon series worked successfully because it was "as much a reinterpretation as a continuation. Although he [Genndy] didn't invent the universe, the vision and the hand were recognizably the animator's."

Some were critical of the show's shortened length. "Everyone wanted them to be longer," Genndy admitted. The network's key demographic, kids, age 6 to 11, were among its biggest fans. One couple reportedly recorded all the episodes as a way to bribe their child to think if he was "good," they would allow him to watch them.

The highest praise came from *Stars Wars* creator George Lucas himself. That weekend, after returning from shooting *Star Wars Episode III: Revenge of the Sith*, he sat down and watched the fast and furious action of the first 10 episodes with his then 10-year-old son Jett and they "were blown away . . . we just loved it. *Clone Wars* is definitely *Star Wars*, but it clearly has Genndy's style. Visually, it's like nothing else out there. . . . It complements the movies well."

6

Changing Directions

Becoming the highest-rated series in its time slot, *Clone Wars* spawned a second season of 10 additional chapters (11–20) on Cartoon Network under Genndy's direction. After producing and directing the first season, he found that working under the limits of three-minute stories helped him learn how to boil down his storytelling to "the most essential bits," unlike *Samurai Jack*—which he continued to produce and direct—that provided a longer form for him to tell the story and yet have the same emotional impact.

Directing short episodes like *Clone Wars*, he discovered that his dialogue had to be much more precise and condensed and say only that which needed to be said. Working with someone else's characters also became a valuable learning experience. As he commented: "It was kind of difficult. For most of my career, I have worked on my own stuff or things I have helped create. This was hard to do justice to someone else's creation."

Unlike the second season, Genndy stated that that first season was "probably the hardest production I've ever been on. . . . Just because of the time crunch that we were on, and the level of difficulty that we had set up for ourselves."

Airing three seasons under Genndy's direction, *Star Wars: Clone Wars* featured many favorite *Star Wars* characters in serialized cartoon form, including Anakin Skywalker, Mace Windu, Obi-Wan Kenobi, C-3P0, and R2-D2. *(Courtesy: Cartoon Network)* © *2003 Lucasfilm Ltd. and TM. All rights reserved.*

Genndy was responsible for introducing a new character into the *Stars Wars* mythology that season: General Grievous, a master strategist and military leader of all the Separatist armies and notorious Jedi killer. His appearance in *Clone Wars* came before his appearance in the big-screen live-action sequel, *Star Wars Episode III*, released months after the series' premiere. Adding the character was done on a fast turnaround. Genndy said he received word from the network, "Hey! George wants you to introduce General Grievous and here's a *little* bit of direction . . . and go!" The series' tight production schedule gave Genndy hardly any time to analyze or develop the character. Lucas's directive was, as Genndy recalled, like, "Okay, he should do this and this, and here's a couple of drawings of him" and "Okay, I like this, this, and this, and okay . . . and it airs in three months."

Nonetheless Genndy was proud to be the first to introduce the galaxy's most ruthless villain. "Introducing the new character of General Grievous is an awesome responsibility," he said at the time. "Working with the great characters of the *Star Wars* universe was humbling to all of us on the crew of *Star Wars: Clone Wars*, but helping to create a new character that will enter the mythology has made us truly feel part of the *Star Wars* family. The fact he is powerful villain made it even cooler."

For the upcoming second season, besides ensuring the series offered plenty of action, Genndy focused more on character development and dialogue. He put in more sequences with Anakin and Obi-Wan Kenobi, or Anakin and Padmé, or General Grievous and Dooku talking, so he could develop their relationships more in the story arcs.

On March 26, 2004, at 9:30 P.M., a new season of *Clone Wars* debuted, beginning with Chapter 11, on Cartoon Network, with subsequent chapters airing from March 29 to April 8 and during a Friday and Saturday marathon on April 9–10. Featuring the continuing battle between Anakin Skywalker and his would-be assassin, the Dark Jedi Asajj Ventress, protégé of the evil Sith lord Count Dooku, Mace Windu takes on an army of Droid soldiers. Meanwhile Yoda undertakes a risky mission to rescue fellow Jedi Barris Offee and Luminara Unduli, who are trapped on the icy planet Ilurn. Joining Yoda in his rescue attempt are Padmé Admidala, C-3PO, and R2-D2.

EARNING THE RESPECT OF HIS PEERS

Genndy's work continued to draw accolades from other industry counterparts. Speaking on the subject of cartooning, *Ren & Stimpy* creator John Kricfalusi noted in an interview with AWN.com in September

2004, "Most cartoons you see today still have garish color; they're pink, purple, and green. Genndy Tartakovsky's cartoons are exceptions—they have great color."

That season Genndy's labor on *Clone Wars* and *Samurai Jack* garnered the respect of his peers. Members of the Academy of Television Arts and Sciences nominated them for prime-time Emmy Awards—for *Samurai Jack* its third Emmy nomination in a row for "Outstanding Individual Achievement in Animation" and for *Clone Wars* its first for "Outstanding Animated Program (For Programming More Than One Hour)."

Clone Wars lost. But after two previous defeats, *Samurai Jack* won. The Emmy was awarded to each of the series' animators—Wes Bane, Derrik Steinhagen, Dan Krall, Scott Willis, and Bryan Andrews—for "Outstanding Individual Achievement in Animation" for their artistic work on the program.

On September 25, 2004, at 7 P.M. (ET and PT), the four-episode finale to Genndy's *Samurai Jack* aired on Cartoon Network after production of the series was halted. In "Seasons of Death," Jack encounters four different menaces as he travels through the four different seasons. In "Tale of X-49," told film noir-style, Aku forces an assassin droid out of retirement to hunt down Jack. "Young Jack in Africa" describes in flashback the foundation of Jack's heroic character, and in "Jack and the Baby," Jack tries to find a lost baby's parents. This swan song, however, provided no definitive conclusion to Jack's overall quest, something many fans found disappointing. The episode was broadcast during Saturday night's *Toonami* action and anime block with a special presentation of all 20 chapters of *Star Wars: Clone Wars*. Even though Cartoon Network originally commissioned 52 half-hour episodes during the show's four-season run and never officially cancelled the series, some episodes aired after the show was cancelled as either specials or reruns. The series was also available for viewings in the United States on Cartoon Network's *Toonami Jetstream* Web site.

The last Emmy nomination for *Samurai Jack*—for the episode "Seasons of Death"—came after the show was off the air for 10 months. "I feel like it's a forgotten show," Genndy said in an interview in August

2005, "so it's great to have it recognized . . . it's the last one that can be nominated, and it's great to see that it did."

Genndy never hid the fact that he always wanted to direct animated features. Finally it appeared he was on his way to fulfilling that desire. In early June 2004, Sony Pictures Entertainment hired him to write and direct its long-in-development film version—after purchasing the film rights in 1997—of the classic Japanese television cartoon series *Astro Boy*.

Based on the character created by Osamu Tezuka, who also created such popular characters as Kimba the White Lion, the *Astro Boy* film, originally set to be a live-action adaptation directed by Eric Leighton (*Dinosaur*) and scripted by Todd Alcott (*Antz*), was halted in 2000 due to its similarities with director Steven Spielberg's science-fiction feature *A.I.* Produced by Don Murphy of Angryfilms and by Lisa Henson and Kristine Belson of Jim Henson Pictures for Sony's Columbia Pictures, this latest version to be directed by Genndy would mix CGI animation, animatronics, and live-action à la the successful *Stuart Little* films. It would mark Genndy's second foray into the competitive feature film arena after directing and producing Cartoon Network's ill-fated feature-length *The Powerpuff Girls Movie*. Unfortunately, despite this promising opportunity, production of the film under Genndy's direction and involvement never materialized. Instead, as announced in the summer of 2006, Hong Kong-based Imagi Animation Studios produced the CGI-animated feature *Astro Boy*, released in October 2009 as part of a three-picture distribution deal with Warner Bros. and The Weinstein Company.

In the meantime Cartoon Network picked up *Clone Wars* for a third season, this time ordering five episodes. This latest installment was to set the stage for the May 19, 2005 theatrical release of the feature-length prequel, *Star Wars Episode III: Revenge of the Sith*. For George Lucas's latest big-screen installment, Genndy also produced the opening scroll story. Working until midnight almost every day of production, it was an opportunity "I couldn't pass up."

The third season of *Clone Wars* was the most challenging out of the three for Genndy to produce and direct. The episodes were longer—12 minutes compared to three. While the preparation was the same regardless of the length, the execution was important. As Genndy related, "We wanted to make sure it was entertaining in all parts. So it was a challenge because people are eventually going to watch it like a movie even though initially they are going to watch it in five segments."

Consequently Genndy had to make fast decisions, stand behind them, and feel good about them in the end. Even then, after the production is all said and done, "you really never get a chance to second-guess yourself," he added.

Prior to the third-season launch of *Clone Wars*, from March 18–19, 2005, Genndy was feted by the American Cinematheque at the Egyptian Theatre with a two-day tribute to his career. The event included screenings of his early film shorts, including rarely seen and unreleased material from his CalArts days, such as "Changes," the basis for his popular Cartoon Network series *Dexter's Laboratory*. Also featured were handpicked episodes of *Samurai Jack*, including the groundbreaking two-parter "Birth of Evil," clips of first season, and world premiere of the entire second season of *Star Wars: Clone Wars*, interstitials he created for Cartoon Network featuring vintage Hanna-Barbera characters. An extended discussion followed after each program with Genndy moderated by animation writer Jon M. Gibson.

From Monday, March 21, to Friday, March 25, the five-episode third season of *Clone Wars* debuted on Cartoon Network. That Saturday, all five episodic shorts were rebroadcast back-to-back. The story picks up from the previous 10 chapters after Anakin Skywalker's defeat of Ventress and Obi-Wan Kenobi's victory on the planet Muunilinst and the Jedi Council's decision to promote Anakin to a knight. Three years later he and Obi-Wan fight to liberate the enslaved and mutated Nelvaanians from the Techno Union in the Outer Rim Territories. General Grievous, meanwhile, heads an assault on Coruscant and kidnaps the Supreme Chancellor Palpatine, angering Anakin who rescues the chancellor with the help of Obi-Wan (corresponding to the starting minutes of the live-action prequel *Star Wars Episode III: Revenge of the Sith*).

For Genndy and his crew, the third season of *Clone Wars* reaped more than high ratings. It walked off with several honors that year—an

Annie Award for "Best Animated Television Production" and two prime-time Emmy Awards for "Outstanding Animation Program (For Programming One Hour or More)" and "Outstanding Individual Achievement in Animation." Genndy also garnered his fourth Emmy nomination for "Outstanding Individual Achievement in Animation" for *Samurai Jack* for the episode, "Seasons of Death."

FULFILLING THE UNFULFILLED—DIRECTING

Fueled by the tremendous success he enjoyed at Cartoon Network, Genndy was ready for new opportunities. It would not be long before he would seize them. Genndy still wanted to make the jump to doing full-length features and something more sophisticated and challenging than television animation. In August 2005, he told *Animation Insider*, "I'm just trying to get some movies going . . . to see if I can get into the theatrical world of feature animation."

Like all great directors, including his heroes Hitchcock, Lean, and Leone, Genndy had developed his own directing style to present his ideas in a more unique and personal way but with a strong point of view. His goal remained one day to make a film that would have audiences say, "Oh, Genndy directed this." Achieving that goal was much too complicated in "a watered down production schedule of television," as he put it.

That October, after making some of television's most acclaimed animated shows, *Dexter's Laboratory*, *The Powerpuff Girls*, *Samurai Jack*, and *Star Wars: Clone Wars*, he set out to do just that. He left the Cartoon Network and accepted the offer to become creative president of the leading San Francisco-based F/X—or visual effects—house, Orphanage Animation Studios. The studio was founded in 1999 by three former artists from George Lucas's special effects division, Industrial Light & Magic, Stuart Maschwitz, Jonathan Rothbart, and Scott Stewart. In his new role, Genndy was charged with the task of spearheading the company's move into producing and directing a slate of full-length animated features.

"After 14 years in TV, I was burned out and wanted to express longer stories and experience them with an audience," Genndy said of his

Genndy is interviewed for a documentary extra for the DVD release of *Star Wars: Clone Wars. (Courtesy: Cartoon Network)* © *2003 Lucasfilm Ltd. and TM.All rights reserved.*

new opportunity. "We'll do family comedies, but we also really want to push action-adventure beyond where it has been."

In joining Orphanage, Genndy brought onboard several top animators from both traditional and CG animation to serve as part of his core team in developing new projects, including the first that he would direct. They included art director and character designer Craig Kellman (whose credits include DreamWorks's hit feature *Madagascar*); former Emmy-winning *Star Wars: Clone Wars* and *Samurai Jack* story artist Bryan Andrews; Emmy-winning *Stars Wars: Clone Wars* art director and background artist Justin Thompson and art director and character designer Paul Rudish; and *SpongeBob SquarePants* and *Samurai Jack* storyboard artist and writer Aaron Springer. Genndy looked at this merging of expertise in visual effects and computer animation as the right recipe for what would form what he called "a unique and fulfilling partnership."

Jumping into the computer-generated film fray, Orphanage, then housed in 18,000-square-feet of office space in the San Francisco Film Centre, joined the Bay Area's digital arts hub that already included Lucasfilm in nearby Presidio, Pixar Animation Studios in Emeryville, DreamWorks Animation in Redwood City, Wild Brain in San Francisco, and CritterPix in San Rafael. Orphanage cofounder and acting chairman Scott Stewart was charged with overseeing business operations of Orphanage's animation studio with Carsten Sorensen and Daniel Gloates serving as CEO and chief financial officer, respectively. The trio was betting that their high-profile hiring of Genndy with his inherent storytelling strengths would help separate them from the pack in a very crowded field. "We view Genndy as our own version of John Lasseter," Sorensen told the *San Francisco Business Times*, referring to Pixar's Academy Award-winning director and creative force. "We didn't want to go out and hire any director. We wanted a creative giant."

Raising hopes that the jump to Orphanage would allow Genndy to do what he always wanted—direct features, Orphanage had secured $20 million from private investors to underwrite development of its films. It was also in negotiations with distributors to secure a distribution deal for feature-film projects, and it was in the process of raising more funds for its productions with its first picture targeted for release in 2008 and new animated films to follow every 18 months thereafter.

Genndy was to direct films budgeted at $50 million to $75 million—much less than $100 million or more for films produced by its two largest competitors, Pixar Animation and DreamWorks Animation. Orphanage planned to employ its experienced creative team and existing tech infrastructure with proven technology used to hone thousands of visual effects shots in numerous blockbuster movies (including *Harry Potter and the Goblet of Fire* and *Superman Returns*) to compete successfully while keeping costs down. Expanding its operations, the company moved into a new facility to accommodate staffing an additional 200 to 300 artists required for CG feature production.

Before making the leap, Genndy had talked to other studios, including Lucasfilm and its Industrial Light & Magic effects house. But in the end, he felt Orphanage provided him the opportunities he sought at this time in his career.

Besides helming the studio's films, Genndy would be responsible for overseeing Orphanage's in-house creative talent in producing future features. Orphanage planned to follow the same path and model that Pixar and others used to forge their way into the feature 'toon arena. They intended to become bigger players in CG animation after principally making their mark as a special effects house like 20th Century Fox's Blue Sky and DreamWorks Animation's PDI (Pacific Data Images) had done. Genndy welcomed the opportunity. As he told a reporter, "Animation is very young. Nobody's pushing the envelope . . . I want to push storytelling and design even further."

As Stewart said in announcing the signing of Genndy, "We don't think that we're going to be successful just because we have a lot of technology. By getting someone like Genndy who has proven himself, we think we separate ourselves from the pack of other startups."

Stewart added that "Our friends across the Bay at Pixar have set the creative bar very high for CG features. We knew if we wanted to achieve that level of quality in our films, we needed a visionary story-teller. We found that storyteller in Genndy. Whether by stepping into George Lucas's shoes to write and direct the acclaimed *Star Wars: Clone Wars* series or by establishing his trademark sense for cinematic action in *Samurai Jack*, Genndy has proven himself to be one of the most innovative and exciting voices in animation today."

Genndy's first feature film marking his directorial debut was to be *The Power of the Dark Crystal*, due out in 2007, for The Jim Henson Company. Set 100 years after the original 1982 blockbuster *The Dark Crystal*, in the sequel, the world has fallen into darkness and a mysterious girl made of fire joins a Gelfling outcast to reignite the dying sun by way of a stolen shard of the legendary Crystal. The film was to be designed by Brian Froud, who had designed the original, and Orphanage Animation was to produce the CG animation for the film in combination with live-action animatronic characters.

A scene from the one of two commercials Genndy directed in 2006 for the stop-smoking product, NiQuitin, for Orphanage Animation Studios.

The Jim Henson Company co-CEO Lisa Henson was delighted over the choice of Genndy to helm the project. As she stated, "As an auteur of such exciting and fantastical adventure projects, Genndy is the perfect director to bring to life *Power of the Dark Crystal*. I am sure that his visualization of Brian Froud's designs will thrill fans of the original film as well as audiences who are meeting these beloved characters for the first time."

The project had everything Genndy had hoped for—including finally being able to direct feature films. As he said, "The original *Dark Crystal* was one of the most inspirational and imaginative pictures of its time, so it's a real honor for me to be able to bring the world of *The Dark Crystal* to a whole new generation."

In addition to working on the film and developing other features, TV series, and pitching commercial work, Genndy and his crew also produced storyboards, designs, backgrounds, and layouts for Orphanage's first production, a five-minute 2-D animated segment in the live-action film *How to Eat Fried Worms*. Opening in theaters nationwide on August 25, 2006, this feature-length adaptation of Thomas Rockwell's popular 1973 young adult book is the story an 11-year-old boy who challenges a class bully on his first day at a new school to eat 10 worms in a single day.

From their Studio City, California, office, Genndy and members of his unit spent the better part of five days churning out the segment that played up the rivalry between the two brothers in the film. Only three minutes of it were used in the final cut of the movie. "This was a huge time restraint and we worked by the seat of our pants," Genndy explained. "There are no iconic illustrations in the book, so we did a '70s *Schoolhouse Rock!*-ish feel."

Of his and Orphanage's involvement in the film, Genndy told AWN.com, "We were asked to make the mood funnier. To say 'it's okay to laugh,' setting a wacky tone in the beginning with the boy throwing up."

That same year Genndy directed a series of antismoking commercials, one for Nicorette in the United States and two years later, two more for NiQuitin in the United Kingdom. In 2006, he also codirected the pilot for a promising new animated television series for Cartoon Network that aired that June on the *Adult Swim* late-night programming block. Created by animation storyboard writer and director Aaron Springer, *Korgoth of Barbaria* was a parody of the *Conan the Barbarian* movies. Production never commenced on a regular weekly series despite a petition drive by fans to revive it.

The directions Genndy had taken thus far in his career soon led him back to his past. It would there that he would discover his future . . . and in a medium that gave him his biggest breakthrough.

7

Back to the Future

After production of his Emmy-winning *Samurai Jack* series ceased, fans were disappointed in its conclusion, feeling no sense of closure after the airing of its final episode. In June 2007, Genndy confirmed that "Jack will come back" and "we will finish the story, and there will be an animated film."

Variety announced that month that Genndy would be writing and directing a feature-length adaptation for Frederator Studios's newly formed production company, Frederator Films. The turn of events came about thanks to Fred Seibert, president of Frederator Studios and Genndy's former boss at Hanna-Barbera Studios. Seibert had written on his blog that he had "watched Genndy grow as a filmmaker from afar, and I remembered Genndy as one of the best people I'd worked with in my entire career. Talented, smart, dedicated, relentless, amazing leader, moral, and fun. What a rare guy."

Seibert arranged to meet Genndy over lunch. He went into it with no expectations. With Genndy concluding a multiyear relationship with George Lucas on *Clone Wars* and having established The Orphanage Animation Studios to develop his own feature films, he was not sure what his company could offer, but on his way to the meeting an opportunity dawned on him on how they could work together. He called Jim

Staples, then-president of Cartoon Network, to grant his company the movie rights to Genndy's hit cartoon series *Samurai Jack*. Samples agreed to grant Seibert the rights so long as Genndy was intimately involved in the project. At the time, Cartoon Network and New Line Cinema had abandoned their plans to produce both animated and live-action films based on the character, and Genndy felt he had let down his fans. The deal took some time to close but, in Seibert's words, "Genndy was thrilled when I delivered the news."

By then Seibert had announced the formation of Frederator Films to branch out into making 2-D animated features budgeted below $20 million. J. J. Abrams, a huge fan of the series, agreed to be Seibert's coproducer on the picture through his company, Bad Robot Productions, at Paramount Pictures. Genndy felt that with Abrams and his producing partner Bryan Burk involved, the project was in good hands and chances had improved of him actually seeing the movie being made and playing in theaters across the country. The *Samurai Jack* project was one of three Frederator had planned to produce along with the clay-animated *The Neverhood*, based on the DreamWorks videogame and written and directed by the game's creator Doug TenNapel, and a hip-hop themed tale, *The Seven Deadly Sins*, featuring the voice of famed boxing promoter Don King. By September of that year, with Genndy directly involved, the film entered preproduction, beginning with writing the script.

Almost four years after its final episode bowed, *Samurai Jack* reappeared on Cartoon Network's *Adult Swim* program block in February 2008, and the first episode of the series was rebroadcast on March 29 during the network's *Toonami* action-adventure and anime block. It continued to air weekly until *Toonami* ceased broadcasting on September 20 of that year.

A month earlier Genndy announced he was returning to his first love—comic books. He would be hitting comic-book shelves with his first comic illustrated for Marvel Comics—a revival of Marvel's hippest hero-for-hire from Harlem and "blaxpoitation" character Luke Cage. Also known as Power Man, the satirical 1970s character would be featured in four brand-new issues. For Genndy, doing the comic-book

Genndy speaks to a flock of science-fiction and fantasy enthusiasts during a panel discussion at the 2009 Comic-Con convention in San Diego.

series was a dream come true. After Marvel editor Aubrey Sitterson met and chatted with Genndy, he came to the realization Genndy was the obvious choice to revive the titular hero.

"You can really tell if you watch a lot of 'Dexter's Lab' episodes, there's a lot of influence from 1970s Marvel properties," said Sitterson, who would be overseeing the project. (Genndy's animated send-up *The*

Justice Friends on *Dexter's Laboratory* was largely influenced by his love of their 1970s comics.)

In lovingly satirizing the Marvel's superhero characters, Genndy's new Luke Cage comics—originally created by writer Archie Goodwin and artist John Romita Sr.—would maintain, as Sitterson announced, that "kitschy, over-the-top, ridiculous Marvel '70s stuff" replete with the character's fan-favorite tiara, mountainous chest hair, open yellow shirt, and big chain belt.

As of September 2010, Genndy had completed writing and drawing thumbnails of each issue. As he stated, "I am so close to finishing it but the time to finish has definitely been an issue. But, it has always been a dream of mine to draw a comic for Marvel and this is my chance, so I promise you I won't let it pass."

By February 2009, Genndy's dreams of directing big-screen features for The Orphanage studios soured. The company announced earlier that month that they were suspending operations indefinitely. Employing 160 people at its peak, Orphanage sold or liquidated its assets with any money going first to pay off creditors. The company shut down everything, including its television commercial unit, except for the Los Angeles-based Orphanage Animation Studios headed by Genndy. It remained open as Genndy continued to work on the studio's first announced feature, *The Power of the Dark Crystal*.

THIRSTING FOR A CHANGE

Genndy still wanted to nurture a project. In his mind, an animated feature seemed like the obvious choice. But with development and financing of such a project taking years to realize from concept to screen, after a few years, "I began to thirst for the quick and exciting pace of television production."

After a more than seven-year hiatus, Genndy announced his return to television animation with a new cartoon series for Cartoon Network to debut in the 2009–2010 season, *Sym-Bionic Titan*. This otherworldly space-opera fantasy stars two alien teens and a robot—plucky Princess

After more than a seven-year hiatus from television, Genndy returned with a brand-new series with his homage to mecha anime action/adventure and robot cartoon shows from the 1970s and 1980s for Cartoon Network, *Sym-Bionic Titan. (Courtesy: Cartoon Network)* © *Cartoon Network*

Ilana, her rebellious soldier protector Lance, and their levelheaded cyborg Octus—who crash-land on Earth after fleeing an evil general who has taken control of their war-torn planet of Galaluna. Afterward, they try blending into everyday life in the fictitious Midwest town of Sherman, Illinois, where they pose as high school students. They do so to conceal their true identify from General Modula and his hideous intergalactic space mutants, the individually armored Galalunans, who are intent on killing them and destroying everything in their wake—from skyscrapers to military battalions. Wearing protective armor, Ilana, Lance, and Octus defend themselves when under attack. But, in extreme times of danger, Octus activates the sym-bionic defense program and the motley trio unite to become one spectacular cyber-giant robot, Sym-Bionic Titan.

Genndy drew inspiration from various mecha anime action and adventure shows he grew up with from the 1970s and 1980s, including *Battle of the Planets*, *Johnny Socko*, *Robotech*, *Spectraman*, *Speed Racer*, *Voltron*, and other Japanese imports. Since his youth, he had always loved the idea of animation of, as he said, "kids driving giant robots." It was a theme he had always played around with, one that was "empowering" and "super cool" to see big robots battle each other.

Three years earlier Genndy started developing the idea but it was much different then. Initially he toyed with creating the show solely about a robot disguised as a human in high school. The entire process of development from concept to premiere took almost two years. He settled on the idea of Octus and the high school setting first, and cocreators Paul Rudish and Bryan Andrews later added Ilana and Lance as protagonists. The character that took the longest time to develop was the female lead, Princess Ilana, who Genndy described as "a positive, strong female character . . . something I've always wanted to create."

Sym-Bionic Titan became the most challenging project he had ever done. Before starting work on the project, like he always does before commencing on a production, Genndy established a list of goals he wanted to achieve. In terms of storytelling, he wanted to make *Sym-Bionic Titan* a character-motivated action, drama, and comedy that intertwined humor with the complexity of teenage life. "After doing *Dexter's Lab* and *Powerpuff Girls*, I felt like we've explored that age 4–12 range of experiences that happens to you as a kid," he said. "Our goal was to focus on themes that were older."

In doing his fourth series, the now 40-year-old animator applied everything he had learned in 16 years of producing and directing television animation since breaking in at age 24. As he explained, "The humor. The action. The way we do the production. It's just the all-out experience cumulating to the new show."

Further influencing his development of the show's fish-out-of-water alien characters was his experience as an immigrant coming to America. Cowriting most of the stories with head writer Darrick Bachman, he based much of what the characters encountered on his real-life experiences, including from his high school days and his difficulty of fitting in as an outsider. He went beyond exploring that theme. Inspired by the character development of Japanese animator Hayao Miyazaki's *Castle in the Sky*, he strove to develop a relationship between the two main characters, Lance and Ilana, based more on camaraderie and friendship than romance. Movies like John Hughes's teen comedies *Sixteen Candles* and *The Breakfast Club* also influenced him in his development of the two teenage leads. "Sometimes it's more difficult to build a friendship than a love relationship," he stated. "Love is easier in a way, because you can always go toward the attraction part. But to have friends be real friends and show them friendly and nice to each other is more complex and that's what inspired me from *Castle in the Sky*."

Genndy strove to push himself and his team to do something new and different visually. He wanted to produce a more drawn and volumetric look but retain some of the design sense they had created in their previous shows. Calling the character design and visual style "a mixed bag of goodies," Genndy credits among his influences in creating the look and direction for his new show the style of *Astro Boy* creator Osamu Tezuka and art director Paul Rudish's original designs. This became more evident to him after seeing other cartoon series on the air produced in the same style of *Dexter's Laboratory, The Powerpuff Girls,* and *Samurai Jack.* "So I started drawing this more Tezuka-ish inspired

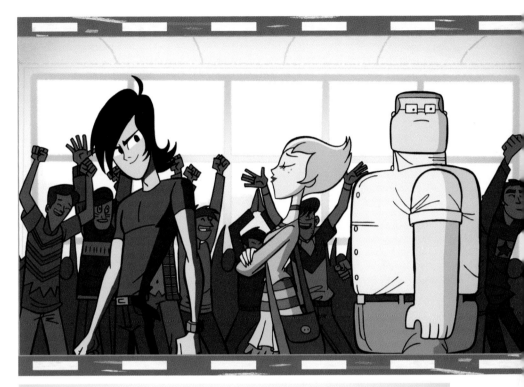

Debuting in 2010, *Sym-Bionic Titans* followed the adventures of two alien teens—the rebellious soldier Lance and plucky Princess Ilana—and their level-headed robot, Octus, who crash-land on Earth in an Illinois suburb after fleeing the war-torn planet of Galaluna. *(Courtesy: Cartoon Network)* © *Cartoon Network*

style . . . a mix between *Speed Racer* and the Fleischer brothers and other Tezuka manga," he said.

Rudish developed the semitranslucent design of the robots adding a Shogun warrior aspect in their creation. The look was accomplished using three-dimensional computer-generated animation with a 2-D rendering process. It was created by the same directors at Rough Draft Studios that worked on *Dexter's Laboratory*, *Clone Wars*, and *Samurai Jack*, to seamlessly blend the characters into the two-dimensional world around them. Genndy proposed the visual style of the character after buying his son, Jacob, a Micronauts toy action figure and watching him play with

Posing as high school students, the war-torn travelers conceal their true identities, ready to defend themselves from the suspected attacks of General Modula and his hideous intergalactic space mutants who want to destroy them. *(Courtesy: Cartoon Network)* © *Cartoon Network*

it. Genndy thought to himself, "Man, this is such a cool thing." Then it struck him: "What if we did a robot that was semitranslucent?"

Consequently Rudish's sleeker and modern design was a pleasant change of pace compared to most futuristic robot-oriented cartoons that were more clichéd. Embodying Tezuka's signature style and old-school anime, the advanced alien look of the main characters and clear exterior of the robots giving way to their complex machinery were groundbreaking and original.

Unlike his martial-arts style action series, *Samurai Jack*, where episodes sometimes featured 15 minutes of fighting, *Sym-Bionic Titan* would offer a better balance between the action of the characters and the story. Due to budgetary constraints, any action was limited to three minutes as "we couldn't have a 10-minute action sequence because we just couldn't afford it," Genndy said. That allowed him and his team to devote more time to progressing the story and determining what else they needed to add to make it exciting and worthwhile. Compared to the nonstop, high action of *Samurai Jack*, he said, "This show has a lot less than that. But we also wanted to develop a really strong character story, dramatic and comedic also. So balancing was hard. So some episodes are heavier toward the action and some are heavier toward the character stuff."

Based on the demands of his new project, Genndy estimated that the pacing of *Sym-Bionic Titan* would be vastly different from his earlier shows. "For Jack there was a lot of opportunity for slower moments where it was one man vs. nature," he explained. "For Titan there are a lot of characters and always multiple story lines so it makes the pacing a bit faster because there is a lot to get through."

Hyped by Cartoon Network as "an exciting hybrid of high school drama and giant robot battles," *Sym-Bionic Titan* premiered on Friday, September 17, 2010 at 8 P.M. (ET and PT). It joined the network's action-packed Friday night lineup that included *Ben 10: Ultimate Alien*, *Batman: The Brave and the Bold*, *Generator Rex*, and *Star Wars: Clone Wars*. A coproduction of Cartoon Network Studios and Orphanage Animation Studios, the pilot episode, titled "Escape to Sherman High," sets the series into motion. A spaceship suddenly crashes in the woods outside of Chicago. Emerging from the misshapen craft is teenage soldier Lance, shape-shifting robot Octus, and the peaceful but naïve Princess Ilana whom they have sworn to protect. With their home planet, Galaluna, under siege, they make Earth their new home disguised as high school students. They make a real effort to navigate high school life while saving Earth and themselves from inter-galactic attacks by General Modula and his Muttradi beasts. As outcasts, they have problems fitting in. Ilana (voiced by Tara Strong) has a hard time meshing with different cliques at school and is labeled a "dweeb" by her peers. Lance (played by Kevin Thoms) faces similar problems. He is bullied by the football team for sitting at their favorite table at lunch. The overly analytical, robotic Octus (voiced by comedian Brian Posehn of TV's *Just Shoot Me*) fares no better. Dressed in a holographic suit, he deadpans, "Apparently the Earthlings consider me a doofus."

Daily Variety critic Brian Lowry likened Genndy's latest series to "a cross between *Gigantor* (for those old enough to remember that) and *Mighty Morphin Power Rangers*—only with better animation than the former, and more brains than the latter." As he added, "Genndy Tartakovsky's *Sym-Bionic Titan* delivers a full-throttle, finely calibrated ride. Drawing from numerous sources, this action-packed, high-school set

Under extreme attack, the motley teenage trio unites to become one spectacular cyber-giant robot, Sym-Bionic Titan, after activating a hidden defense program. *(Courtesy: Cartoon Network) © Cartoon Network*

Cartoon Network entry should score a bull's-eye with boys and tweens.
. . . About all that's missing is a pithy catchline and pronounceable title."
In reviewing the premiere, Scott Thill of Underwire.com stated: "Tarta-
kovksy's Sym-Bionic Titan is another masterful hybrid of international
animation styles and substances that, like his acclaimed former series,
appeals broadly across demographics . . . Sym-Bionic Titan instantly
transforms into an adult-oriented intergalactic smackdown that levels
everything from skyscrapers to military battalions in its action-packed
path."

Sym-Bionic Titan produced huge overnight ratings in its prime-time
debut. The first episode attracted 1.738 million viewers and posted
strong double-digit growth across all targeted kids and boys demographics versus the same time period from the previous year. Initially
Cartoon Network ordered 20 episodes, and 11 half-hours were broadcast through December.

During this period, Genndy's development of a *Samurai Jack* feature film for producer J. J. Abrams's company, Bad Robot, was ongoing.
In October 2010, it was still in the writing and development phase, usually a long process in developing a feature-length project. Genndy completed another outline of the story and had received positive feedback.
"We'll do revisions and hopefully we can actually start storyboarding,"
he told AWN.com in an interview that month. "It's on the cusp of going
to full greenlight, but we're not quite there yet."

In his heart, Genndy still desired to do live-action feature projects.
Although *The Power of Dark Crystal*, in his words, "fit perfectly," outside
of storyboarding *Iron Man 2*, which "really made me love animation
more," nothing had come along that struck his fancy. For the time being
he was content, saying, "I definitely know inside my gut that I'm an animator and I love animation and I love drawing. I really missed it when
I wasn't doing that."

Genndy's work on *Iron Man 2* evolved after he tried to sell an animated project to Marvel. The studio executive he met with asked, "Have
you ever met Jon Favreau?"

"No," Genndy answered.

Genndy learned the big differences between animation and live-action filmmaking while working on *Iron Man 2* and *The Power of the Dark Crystal*. (Photo by Mark Hill/Courtesy: Cartoon Network)

So the executive arranged for the two of them to meet. They got together for lunch to talk about different ideas. At one point Favreau gushed about how much he liked *Clone Wars* and *Samurai Jack*, especially the fight scenes. Then he asked if Genndy would like to help on the *Iron Man* sequel. He agreed and, along with Bryan Andrews, started storyboarding the film, including the entire Expo and Japanese garden action sequence.

Stylistically, for a live-action film, the boards Genndy created were much more realistic looking than for a wholly animated production, yet drawn in a cartoony style. However, with live-action requiring far more shots than animation and the execution therefore more expensive, he found himself thinking more economically in his approach. As he explained, "I had to think of the real world. I was storyboarding this highway chase sequence and I actually went to the location and took a bunch of pictures and laid it out and kind of walked myself through it to see how I would actually shoot it. So it's a very different experience because before I would think of a picture and I would just draw it."

Genndy's imprint in the mediums of animation and television has hardly been ordinary. Amassing 13 Emmy nominations (and counting) and four awards and one Annie Award out of four additional nominations in his career, he has proven he belongs. Like the old soul he is, his success is the result of old-fashioned values: from hard work and diligence. No matter how hard the prospects or how difficult the challenge, he never gave up on his goals, much less on himself. He followed his heart knowing there was only one place for him—the world of animation.

Tapping his potential, Genndy has left his mark. He has lived up to his calling, producing laughter, thrills, and excitement for children and adults around the globe. His timeless characters and programs have become classics in their time and continue to delight audiences. He is a modern-day legend in the making. Using his pen and his imagination, he has come of age.

SELECTED RESOURCES

For further study of Genndy Tartakovsky's work and career, the following resources are recommended:

FILMOGRAPHY

Genndy Tartakovsky Filmography (http://www.imdb.com/name/nm0850733/filmotype)

This filmography provides titles, credits, release dates, and synopses of every production from Tartakovsky's career.

DVD & VIDEO COLLECTIONS

Dexter's Laboratory: Season One (Cartoon Network, 2010)

This two-disc set contains 13 22-minute episodes of Tartakovsky's first hit series for Cartoon Network, including two *Dexter* cartoons and one alternating supporting cartoon of *Dial M for Monkey* and *The Justice Friends* per program.

The Powerpuff Girls 10th Anniversary Collection: The Complete Series (Turner Home Entertainment, 2009)

This amazing six-disc collection features all 78 episodes and the *T'was the Fight Before Christmas* special starring creator Craig McCracken's superpowered girl trio Blossom, Bubbles, and Buttercup from the Emmy award-wining Cartoon Network series that Tartakovsky animated.

Star Wars: Clone Wars, Volume 1 (20th Century Fox Home Video, 2005)

Featured in this first DVD volume are the first 20 chapters of George Lucas's animated micro-series that Tartakovsky directed. It includes a behind-the-scenes featurette including interviews with Lucas, Tartakovsky, and the *Clone Wars* production crew.

Star Wars: Clone Wars, Volume 2 (20th Century Fox Home Video, 2005)

This second volume picks up where Volume 1 left off, comprised of five 12-minute chapters (21–25) rather than three-minute chapters as in the first *Clone War* series, again under Tartakovsky's direction. The disc includes numerous bonus features, among them an exclusive *Connecting the Dots* featurette taking fans inside the creative process that Tartakovsky and his production team used in making the series.

Samurai Jack: Seasons 1–3 (Turner Home Entertainment, 2006)

This set contains all 39 episodes of Tartakovsky's futuristic samurai and cinematic-styled Emmy Award-winning series, starting with the 90-minute 2001 trilogy movie.

SELECTED
BIBLIOGRAPHY

Adams, Thelma. "Questions for Genndy Tartakovsky: The Big Draw." *The New York Times Magazine*, August 19, 2001, 17.

Brodesser, Claude. "'Astroboy' Takes Off." *Daily Variety*, June 2, 2004.

Bynum, Aaron H. "Interview with Genndy Tartakovsky." *Animation Insider*. August 29, 2005. Available online. URL: http://www.anima tioninsider.net/article.php?articleID=838.

Cruz, Gilbert. "Star Wars: Clone Wars." *Entertainment Weekly*, March 25, 2005, Issue 812.

DeMott, Rick. "Genndy Tartakovsky Takes on Giant Robots." AWN .com, October 21, 2010. Available online. URL: http://www.awn.com/articles/article/genndy-tartakovsky-takes-giant-robots.

Epstein, Daniel Robert. "Genndy Tartakovsky Talks 'Samurai Jack.' UGO .com. Available online. URL: http://www.ugo.com/channels/dvd/fea tures/samuraijack_season1/genndytartakovsky.asp.

Fost, Dan. "Orphanage Shoots for Computerized Feature Films." *The San Francisco Chronicle*, October 19, 2005.

Frick, Lisa. "Genndy Tartakovsky." *Newsmakers*, September 1, 2004.

Fritz, Ben. "Fine-Tooning Movies: Cartoon Net Animator Home at Orphanage." *Daily Variety*, October 11, 2005.

Gates, Anita. "TV Weekend." *The New York Times*, August 10, 2001, E. 1:29.

"Genndy Tartakovsky." Sci-Fi Online, March 18, 2005. Available online. URL: http://www.sci-fi-online.com/Interview/05-03-18_GenndyTarta kovsky.htm.

"Genndy Tartakovsky to Direct 'Power of the Dark Crystal.'" The Jim Henson Company, February 1, 2006.

Goldstein, Debra. "Spotlight on Career: Lab Animator." *Science World,* November 15, 1996.

Haithman, Diane. "Morning Report: Arts and Entertainment." *The Los Angeles Times,* November 24, 2001, F. 2.

Holden, Stephen. "They Have a Tantrum, Then Save the World." *The New York Times,* July 3, 2002, E. 3.

"In Toon With Tots." *People,* March 3, 1997, Vol 47, Issue 8.

Itzkoff, Dave. "Free to Follow His Heart Right Back to 'Star Wars.'" *The New York Times,* June 29, 2008, AR 1.

Kissell, Rick. "Summer Sampler: 'Samurai Jack.'" *Daily Variety,* June 8, 2001, Vol. 272, Issue 5.

Linan, Steven. "Tuned In: 'Samurai Jack' Knows the Score." *The Los Angeles Times,* August 10, 2001, F. 32.

Lloyd, Robert. "'Television Review: *Clone's*' New Reality: The Cartoon Network Series at Least Has the Decency to Look Like the Caricature It's Ultimately Become." *The Los Angeles Times,* October 3, 2008, E. 28.

Lowry, Brian. "Television Reviews: Sym-Bionic Titan." *Daily Variety,* September 17, 2010.

Mallory, Michael. "Leaping Into Action; Cartoon Network Takes a Chance on 'Samurai Jack,' an Animated Series That Spans Times, Places and Genres." *The Los Angeles Times,* August 30, 2001, F. 34.

Mifflin, Lawrie. "A Cartoon Winner." *The New York Times,* April 24, 1996, C.18.

Mitchard, Jacquelyn. "A Dandy Dexter." *TV Guide,* July 3, 1996, Vol. 44, Issue 29, 30.

Moore, Scott. "Creative 'World Premiere Toons.'" *The Washington Post,* February 26, 1995, Y. 60.

———. "Expanded Favorites a Boon for Toons." *The Washington Post,* July 13, 1997, Y. 7.

———. "Kid Concocts 'Dexter Laboratory." *The Washington Post,* April 26, 1998, Y. 6.

———. "TV Cartoon Network Goes to the Girls." *The Washington Post,* January 17, 1999, Y. 6.

———. "Attack of the Cartoons; 'Star Wars' Series Fills Void Between Movies." *The Washington Post,* November 6, 2003, C. 14.

Nichols, Judy. "Worth Noting on TV." *The Christian Science Monitor,* April 26, 1996, 15.

"The Orphanage Shuts Down." *Filmmaker Magazine,* February 5, 2009. Available online. URL: http://www.filmmakermagazine.com/blog/2009/02/orphanage-shuts-down.php.

Reuben, Bryan. "Dexter's Laboratory." *Chemistry and Industry,* October 5, 1998.

Sanders. Andrienne. "Orphanage Seeks Home for 300 Jobs." *San Francisco Business Times,* October 15, 2005.

Seymour, Gene. "Movie Review: No Hands and No Feet, But 'Powerpuff Girls' Have Plenty of Wit." *The Los Angeles Times,* July 3, 2002, F. 10.

Shattuck, Kathryn. "A Strong, Silent Type in a Changing World." *The New York Times,* September 23, 2001, 13, 63.

Snider, Mike. "'Star Wars' Goes Animated Tonight." *USA Today,* November 7, 2003.

Solomon, Charles. "Television & Radio: The Light Side of the Force." *The Los Angeles Times,* November 7, 2003, E. 31.

Weinstein, Steve. "The New 'Toons: Keep 'em Short—Today's New Animators Have Returned to the Six-Minute Short." *The Los Angeles Times,* February 20, 1995, 1.

Wilkinson, Alec. "Moody Toons: The King of the Cartoon Network." *The New Yorker,* May 27, 2002.

Winclechter, Dan. "Genndy Tartakovsky Returns with Sym-Bionic Titan." AmbienceofMedia.com, March 25, 2009. Available online. URL: http://www.ambienceofmedia.com/2009/03/25/genndy-tartakovsky-returns-with-sym-bionic-titan.

Wineman, Daniel. "Never Underestimate the Power of a Puff." *The New York Times,* November 15, 1998, 13, 59.

"The Year 2002; TV's Best." *The New York Times,* January 12, 2003, 4.

INDEX

ABOUT THE AUTHOR

Photo courtesy: Brian Maurer.

Jeff Lenburg is an award-winning author, celebrity biographer, and nationally acknowledged expert on animated cartoons who has spent nearly three decades researching and writing about this lively art. He has written nearly 30 books—including such acclaimed histories of animation as *Who's Who in Animated Cartoons*, *The Great Cartoon Directors*, and four previous encyclopedias of animated cartoons. His books have been nominated for several awards, including the American Library Association's "Best Non-Fiction Award" and the Evangelical Christian Publishers Association's Gold Medallion Award for "Best Autobiography/Biography." He lives in Arizona.